HISTORIC DENVER

*This publication was made possible through
the generous cooperation of
The First National Bank of Denver
Colorado's oldest financial institution founded in 1860.*

HISTORIC DENVER

The Architects and The Architecture
1858-1893

by Richard R. Brettell

 A Publication of Historic Denver, Inc.

Second Printing April 1979

Comtemporary Photographs by Bart Edwards
Assisted by Susan Brown

Design and Composition by
Graphic Impressions

———————————————

Copyright by Historic Denver, Inc. 1973
Library of Congress Catalog Card Number: 73-90016
International Standard Book Number: 0-914248-00-6
Printed in United States of America

Published by Historic Denver, Inc.

Introduction

The purpose of *Historic Denver* is to entertain, to inform, and, most importantly, to arouse the people of twentieth century Denver to an awareness of the architecture which made Denver one of America's great nineteenth century cities. Many of these buildings still stand, giving the Denver of today a depth of character and a breadth of identity. The purpose of *Historic Denver* is also to encourage preservation, for this architectural heritage is dwindling— in part because of a lack of knowledge, but also because of a conflict in values. Development, economy, renewal, modernity and "progress," often without much thought, result in the destruction of popular and adaptable older buildings and even whole neighborhoods. Thus a city can lose its heart.

Commissioned by Historic Denver, Inc., this book is dedicated to the people of Denver and to a cause which can make Denver a great twentieth century city. Legislation, funding, interest and hard work are essential to save the city's architectural heritage, so that our children and their children can experience the personality, the color and the character of Denver's past.

There is always a story behind a book and for the sake of history this one should be mentioned. Historic Denver, Inc. was organized late in 1970, with preservation of the Molly Brown House as its first objective. From the outset, however, members admired the books published in other cities to record the architectural past, and envied the preservation activity which such books inspired. Members were also encouraged by the local preservation activity of many other organizations and individuals, including the Junior League of Denver (which in 1966 began the first Denver survey of buildings of architectural interest), the Denver Landmark Preservation Commission, the Colorado State Historical Society, the Colorado Council on the Arts and Humanities, the National Trust for Historic Preservation, the local liaison and advisory personnel for the National Register of Historic Places, the Denver Planning Office (which is now engaged in a comprehensive architectural survey), and many others. Thus, early in 1972 a book of this sort, or perhaps a series of books, became an important objective of Historic Denver, Inc.

In November of 1972 a publications committee was formed, consisting of Cal Cleworth and Dorothy Roberts, publishers; Don Etter, author; and Dana Crawford, preservationist. The committee's goals included publication during 1973. In March of 1973 the committee engaged Rick Brettell, who had done extensive research on Denver architects and architecture of the period 1858-1893, to write the text. He possesses an educated eye, nimble style and a unique point of view. Contemporary photography was provided primarily by Bart Edwards and Susan Brown, but also by Don Etter, Ken Watson and Colorado's well known Jim Milmoe. Historic photographs and other illustrations came from private files and the oustanding collections of the Western History Department of the Denver Public Library and the Colorado State Historical Society. Liz Steinbeck and the staff of Graphic Impressions worked long, hard and creatively on the seldom lauded tasks of design and layout, and Elizabeth Imig was a tireless editor. Thanks to the efforts of these and others, the committee's deadline has been met and, we hope, Historic Denver, Inc.'s purposes served.

It's now up to the people of Denver. Preservation is for the people.

Contents

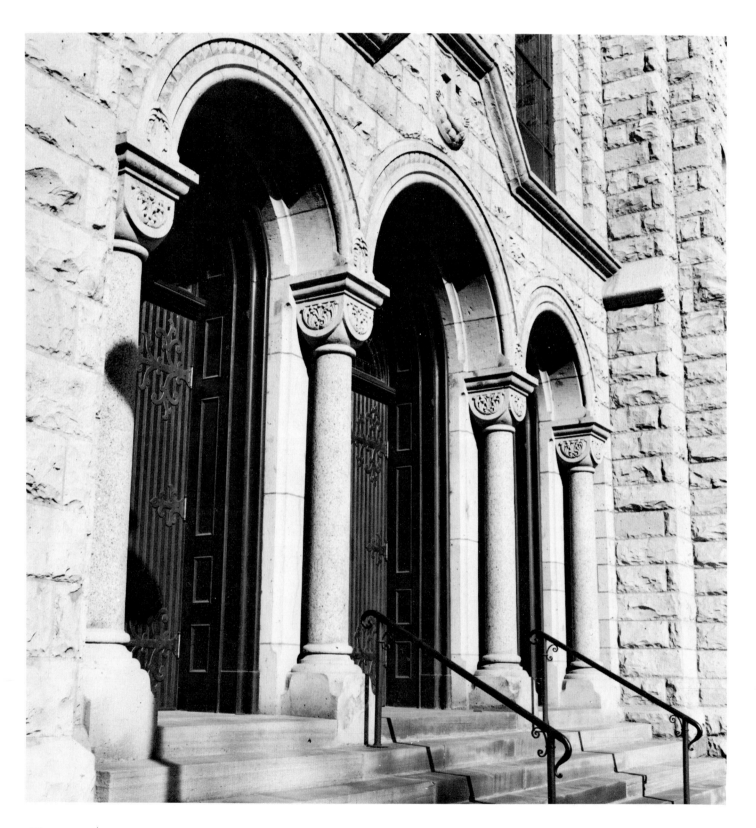

Foreword

Architecture constitutes our most visible past. We live in old buildings, walk down old sidewalks, drive along streets which were laid out by our ancestors, and play in old parks. Cities are, in many ways, archeological remains which are continually maintained and restored, and life within the confines of a city is a perennial effort to renew and extend its physical remains. We are surrounded by our own past in architectural form, and all architecture, no matter how "modern" and how seemingly maintenance-free, requires both use and care to survive.

In the face of new growth in this century, Denver has been careless of its past. A few buildings have been saved: Larimer Street in the 1400 Block, 9th Street in Auraria, the Molly Brown House, and the block of Humbolt Street between 10th and 11th, and several additional nineteenth century structures, mostly churches, have been placed on the National Register of Historic Places. But as was made obvious by the destruction of the Moffat mansion, there are limits to what the preservationist can do. Denver needs a more secure and a more realistic knowledge of her own past before it is totally warped by the racy and irresponsible pioneer image, an image which has dominated our understanding of nineteenth century Denver and the entire Rocky Mountain west for too many years.

Denver architecture was not unique in the nineteenth century, nor was there a pronounced regional style which developed in the city. Denver was designed, like most of the great midwestern cities of the nineteenth century, by its own architects and financed almost completely from within the state. It competed for national dominance with other large midwestern cities, and its aesthetic impetus came primarily from Chicago and Minneapolis. The architecture of Chicago is well-known today because of the preeminence of Frank Lloyd Wright in the twentieth century and the scholarship which attempts to explain the genesis of the skyscraper in American architecture. Minneapolis is much less well-known. It, like Denver, has never been particularly careful of its past, and its architectural reputation has suffered. The architecture of these three cities— and probably Omaha, Salt Lake City, and Kansas City as well— forms a viable whole and is deserving of serious scholarship to define it. All the cities were constructed in the latter decades of the nineteenth century, mostly in the 1880's; all the cities were designed by architects and constructed during building booms; Denver, Chicago, and Minneapolis produced noteworthy architectural magazines in their periods of greatest growth, and all of them exhibited undeniable aesthetic connections. Late and wild eclecticism flourished in all of them and was joined by a sober and simple architecture deriving both from the rigors of commercial design and from the massive-walled architecture of Henry Hobson Richardson designed in the 1880's. These types of architecture developed side by side and arose from the same conditions. Eclecticism was predominantly a domestic style, while Richardsonianism was an institutional and commercial style. There were, of course, many over-lappings and confusions between these two styles, and the cross-currents produced some of the most interesting and least "pure" architecture in the history of that art.

This book traces in some detail the architecture of Denver in its most exciting and prolific years, 1879 to 1893. The architecture of the sixties and seventies is touched on, but is not described in detail or treated with much definitive intention. The early architecture is described only to give background for what I believe to be the most important period in the history of the city, the decade and a half which preceded the silver crash of 1893.

Denver as we know it today was conceived and built in that period; its era of greatest expansion and cultural optimism was during that period; and it harbored many of its greatest architects in that period. Literally thousands of buildings were constructed in the building boom of the later eighties and early nineties; over 25,000 structures standing today pre-date the year 1911. Obviously, only a select few of those buildings can be treated in this text. Omitted from careful consideration are some of my favorite buildings by some of my favorite architects. The Kittredge building, one of the few notable late nineteenth century structures remaining in downtown Denver, is not treated seriously in the text, nor is its architect, A. M. Stuckert. William Quayle, the architect of the presently endangered Ashland School (formerly the North Side High School), is also practically ignored. Simplicity and clarity were chosen as preferable to encyclopedic completeness, and a great many buildings of some note are simply not included in the book.

In writing this book for Historic Denver, Inc., I took a serious look at the recent group of civic architectural histories published in the United States. I have used none of these books as a model. I have avoided the "this is what we have left" approach which characterizes the book on San Francisco entitled *Here Today*. I have also avoided separating "history" from "architecture," a separation deftly made in the recent book on Portland, Maine. A neighborhood by neighborhood approach, around-the-corner-and-next-door architectural history, has also been avoided. What I have tried to do is to give the general reader, the reader with no knowledge of architectural history, an account of the major events and the major people in the history of Denver architecture until 1893.

This architectural picture of Denver in those active years before the silver crash is sometimes evasive. Most architects persistently avoided the public eye and left no traces except listings in the *Denver Directory* or the *Western Architect and Building News*. For others, like Edbrooke and Roeschlaub, careers are reasonably well-described but very little biographical information exists. The problems are manifold, and it seems strange that men who were responsible for building a great and beautiful city have disappeared so completely.

Although the lack of nineteenth century sources has been a problem, it has been more than off-set by present citizens of Denver who have encouraged me in my work, who have given me valuable information, and who have taught me to love Denver today as much as I cherish nineteenth century Denver. For assistance in research and acquisition of photographs, the staff of the Western History Department in the Denver Public Library has been invaluable. I would like particularly to thank Jim Davis, who spent months patiently guiding me through the riches of the photograph collection at the Denver Public Library. Mrs. Alice Sharp of the State Historical Society was also very helpful and allowed me access to the drawings and plans of nineteenth century buildings in the museum's vaults.

Viola Huddart Westbrook and H. H. Baerresen lent me valuable and unique volumes of their fathers' work for photographic reproduction and gave previously unpublished and obscure information. G. Meredith Musick and Alan Fisher provided extremely helpful architectural criticism and information, and Kenneth Fuller gave me access to his valuable archival work in late nineteenth century Denver architecture.

In addition I would like to express deep gratitude to Don and Carolyn Etter, John and Dana Crawford, and Robert David Farmer for their substantive criticism of the book and their personal friendship and concern. Countless other people aided in the conception or completion of this book. Dottie Roberts, Cal Cleworth, Ken Watson, Rosalie Mier, Susan Brown, John L. Gray, Elizabeth Schlosser, Margaret Cloonan, Anne Kerkman, and Kathy Renner were all of great assistance. Elizabeth Imig as editor and Elizabeth Steinbeck as designer supplied immeasurable help, and Bart Edwards gave generously of his talents as photographer.

The most personal thanks goes to the members of my family, who had to live with me during the intensive periods of preparation and writing— my parents, Dr. and Mrs. H. R. Brettell; my sisters, Lisa, Leslie and Laurie; my grandmother, Mrs. Charles E. Hegewald; and my wife Carol. Without their support the book could never have been written.

Richard R. Brettell
Denver, 1973

Precise dating of Denver's nineteenth century architecture is difficult. Sources frequently disagree on the year of construction, the laying of the cornerstone, and even the opening of a building, and architects themselves dated their buildings in no consistent manner. In the *Western Architect and Building News,* for example, some architects included their designs from the project stage and others listed only buildings actually under construction.

As a general rule, dating in an architectural history is looser than dating in political or social history. Events are points in time, whereas buildings require a commission, a design process, a period of construction, and often alterations to correct technical, aesthetic or structural problems which arise after the actual plan is completed. Wherever possible in this book, the date is of the design rather than the opening date or completion of construction. However, the paucity of primary sources makes many buildings, especially those constructed before the mid-eighties, impossible to date with precision.

R. R. B.

Denver's Architectural Growth, 1858-1893

The Founding of the City

The Initial Years
1858–1870

The romantic desire to depict a pioneer past filled with violence, lawlessness, immorality, and a kind of primitive lustiness has triumphed in most descriptions of the early years of Denver. The rough, tough, overtly masculine pioneer image which so fascinated westerners of the nineteenth century continues to obsess many modern students of this period.

Although this picture of the city is not totally inaccurate, it has been greatly exaggerated. There *were* hangings, shootings, drunken performances, and plenty of practical jokes, as dutifully noted by the manifold historians of early western culture. There were also middle-class merchants, churches, schools, families, and all the rest that accompanied small-town life in nineteenth century America. The respectable citizens committed their small fortunes, their lives, and their talents to brick, wood, and stone and constructed what must have been, in spite of occasional flare-ups from the rowdy crowd, a relatively sleepy, dry, and normal town on the great plains.

Nineteenth century Denver began, as did most western towns, rather inauspiciously and awkwardly. Its founding at the confluence of the South Platte River and Cherry Creek occurred sometime in 1858, and before long three little towns— Auraria, Denver City, and the short-lived St. Charles City— began to compete for dominance. The best characterization of the founding of the three towns which later became the city of Denver was written somewhat before the turn of the century by Jerome C. Smiley.

"Denver's founding was an accident of circumstances at a time when even the circumstances bid fair to be transitory, and when advantages and resources may be said to have been unknown. In her infancy, she was the temporary objective point for thousands who cared nothing for the country, nothing for the town; who had no intention of permanently identifying themselves with either and with but the one thought of getting what they came for before somebody else got it, and then getting away again. It was not until the rare beauty of the accidental location, the grandeur of the region, the charms of the climate, and the enormous permanent resources of the country became fixed in the minds of the people, that these alien feelings and purposes disappeared."[1]

The first few years of the 1860's were unstable and rather loose years in the history of Denver. Buildings were cheap, wooden, and temporary. Early inhabitants came and went with great abandon, and the city had a relatively large temporary population. The early houses of Denver were cabins, not built to last for long and ineffective at keeping out the rain and the cold.[2]

Cottonwood and willow logs cut from trees along the banks of the river apparently provided materials for several hundred cabins in the late 1850's and early 1860's. The first cabins were about fifteen by twenty feet, constructed of large, unhewn logs and with a centrally raised gable. The space between the logs was filled with smaller pieces of wood and plaster clay, and the entire structure was usually roofed with earth. These earthen roofs proved a disaster. They became saturated during rainstorms and dripped muddy water into the interior of the cabin, often for weeks after the initial storm. When E.P. Stout, the president of the Denver Town Company, built his small cabin, he roofed it with the pieces of two large tents— a solution which was an

owntown Denver in the early 1860's.

improvement in a rainstorm but was not satisfactory for the cold winter months. In 1859, four months after the construction of his cabin and after the winter of 1858-59, Stout ordered pine shingles and rough sawed lumber for the first proper roof in the city of Denver.

Denver architecture of the late fifties and early sixties was hardly architecture at all. The city's initial inhabitants wanted cheap, temporary shelter and were not concerned with establishing a permanent and long-lived settlement. The businesses established in those early years were clustered close to both rivers on what was known as Indian Row, and the residential cabins were spread about spaciously either out of a desire for privacy or in hopeful anticipation of a building boom.

The situation had changed somewhat by the autumn of 1860. A watercolor of Larimer Street done in that year depicts a scene typical of Colorado boom towns in the 1860's and 1870's. The buildings, long wooden sheds with false fronts, had raised porches which served as wooden sidewalks. They were crowded together protectively and possessed a faint urbanity lacking in the free-standing log cabins of the pioneer era. These were buildings for a more established commercial economy; they were conceived as a group and formed the first real street in Denver's history. Although built exclusively of wood, they had an undeniable architectural presence.

As the pursuit of carelessness and irresponsibility which characterized the antics of the urban fringe in the 1860's was countered by a new sobriety, the log cabins of the late 1850's were pulled down with increasing frequency to make room for the new buildings of brick and planed wood.

The Brick: Commercial and Institutional Architecture of the 1860's

Among the first and the most fortunate natural advantages noticed by the enterprising early citizens of Denver was the presence of large quantities of brick clay. The *Rocky Mountain News* talked grandly about the abundance of brick clay in 1859, and Denver's first brick building, a powder house for Laflin, Smith, and Company, was constructed early in the autumn of that same year. Brick houses appeared in both Denver and Auraria early in 1860, and by the middle of that year bricks were advertised as cheaper than wood.

Denver's brick clay was found in pockets almost immediately adjacent to the city. Bricks were made in local brick yards, and almost no money was spent on importation. In spite of the initial abundance of trees on the shores of the two "rivers," wood must have been scarce by the early 1860's. Transporting large logs from the mountains to Denver was very costly before the introduction of the railroad, and brick increasingly

Stout cabin, 17th and Larimer Streets, 1858.

Larimer Street, watercolor photograph, 1860.

View of Larimer Street in the later 1860's.

proved to be a good, cheap, available and durable building material. By the middle of the decade, almost all new buildings constructed in the city limits were built of brick.[3]

Fires and floods occurred frequently, and wooden structures often failed to survive these disasters. After the fire of 1863 construction of new frame buildings was prohibited in the business district, and the even greater fire of 1864 induced many people to build brick houses as well. Certainly by the middle of the 1860's, Denver was a brick city.

The city of Denver the day after the Cherry Creek flood, May 19, 1864.

Another aspect of early Denver history which undoubtedly affected the city's architectural climate was the attitude of the citizens toward Indians. Except for the usually peaceful Arapahoes, after whom Denverites named their first real school in the early seventies, the Indians were a source of great fear to Denverites. Indian raids of the 1860's enhanced this fear, which was as important as the fear of fire and flood in influencing the brick architecture of the 1860's. The early desire to constrict the size of the city, to band together, and to avoid the use of any wood on the exterior of the building was clearly related to the fear of Indian attack, as possibly was the spare, unornamented cubicity of most Denver buildings which date from the 1860's. Windows were often rather small, and some early photographs of interiors display a suspiciously large number of gun racks, often in the dining room.

Denver's streets had a remarkable grandeur and urbanity in the late 1860's. The buildings were solid and well-built, and the warm orange-red of the brick was attractive on the parched, treeless plains. The city was making a self-conscious attempt to become law-abiding and secure, and this movement was reflected in the city's architecture. The tallest building was the Lawrence Street Church, in the perpendicular gothic mode popular in the United States in the 1840's and 1850's.[4] Its spire and the pinnacles which sprang from the buttresses stood in confident splendor above the brick arches at street level. Denver's other tall and greatly admired structure was the Colorado Seminary, at the corner of Arapahoe and 14th Streets. This large two-story brick block had gables on all four facades, a prominent attic level, and a crowning cupola in the center.

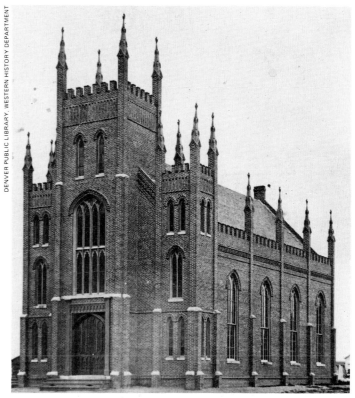

Architect Unknown/Lawrence Street Methodist Church, 1864 —demolished.

Clark, Gruber & Co. Bank and Mint, 16th and Market Streets, 1860–demolished.

The predominant imagery of Denver in the 1860's consisted of red brick arches, repetitive bay construction, restrained brick cornices, and relatively inert silhouettes, reflecting the nature of the city: established, self-consciously urban, and independent. No longer a city based solely on the patronage of miners and travelers who came through seeking temporary shelter and a little "fun," Denver attracted people who came to the west to establish new lives rather than to make quick fortunes, and who yearned for a stable and secure existence.

During the 1860's women began to assume a dominant role in Denver society, and the construction of homes was a major portion of the city's burgeoning building trade. In addition, lots within the urban core of Denver, an area which included Blake, present-day Market, and Larimer Streets between the river and 16th Street, filled up completely by the middle of the decade, and by 1867 even 15th Street and the less developed 16th and 17th Streets began to assume a commercial character to some degree.

The decade of the 1860's, however, can be characterized more as a decade of improvement than of expansion. The population of the city in 1867 included only 3,500 permanent residents, a figure which did not represent a considerable increase since the beginning of the decade. Instead of spreading the new city outward, Denver citizens of the middle part of the decade tore down the old buildings, many of which had been rendered useless by fire or flood damage, and replaced them with better buildings. Only hints of the city's suburbs which developed later in the century were noticeable in the 1860's. Highlands consisted of several farm houses, and Capitol Hill included two smallish brick residences built in 1865.

The architecture of the 1860's was anything but exuberant and exciting. Buildings were constructed of one material, in one color, and with few exceptions in one style. Although they had a certain resemblance to the early Victorian architecture of the east coast at the time of their construction, they must be seen as a regularization and a simplification of that architecture. Early Denver was virtually isolated until the arrival of the railroad in 1870. Mail was slow, and contact with the east coast was infrequent and tentative. The city had no public or private library of any stature until well into the 1880's. Magazines which arrived from the east coast were illustrated with linocuts of a remarkably bland character, often done from drawings by good artists but transferred to the wood-block by skilled but uninspired technicians. Photography, which became the dominant

Larimer Street in 1865 from a sketch by A. E. Mathews published in his Pencil Sketches of Colorado, *1866.*

mode of periodical reproduction later in the century, had not been adapted to printing at that time, and Denver's own photographers showered the city in self-images. Denverites, in short, lived in an extremely localized world, dominated by their own problems and their often greatly exaggerated fears.

Denver's architecture expressed its cultural isolation with an amazing clarity and success, and the buildings of Denver in the 1860's had a simplicity and compactness which did not succumb to the tendency to over-decorate or revel in complexity and pomposity.

In spite of the uniformity of Denver architecture of the 1860's, it is possible to discuss the commercial architecture separately from the residential and institutional architecture.

Denver's best commercial architecture can be called classical in character despite the use of segmental arches on the upper floors. The street facades displayed a distinct regularity and periodicity. They generally lacked a central feature which would give the facade a dramatic or Palladian character, and they never affected the heavy cornices which projected from the facade in buildings constructed after the arrival of the railroad. As constructed objects, they derived a great deal of their character from the brick of which they were constructed. The arches were brick, the cornices were brick, and, of course, the walls were brick. The bricks were the

same size and the same color throughout the 1860's, and their uniformity must have been a key factor both in the regularization and the uniformity of the buildings constructed with them. The brick industry, very lucrative in the small city of the 1860's, had very little sophistication in those years. Bricks were not designed and specified by the architect of the building as they were in later years— architects did not exist in Denver of the 1860's. Rather, both buildings and bricks were designed by the contractors and brick-layers who built the buildings, and the uniformity of design and construction materials is obviously attributable to the existence of a small group who created the buildings from parts manufactured in the city.

The outstanding commercial building of the 1860's was the Brendlinger Block at the corner of 15th and Blake Streets, a two-story brick building which had an arcade-like row of identical rounded arches on the ground floor.[5] The second floor was divided into bays corresponding exactly to the arches below, each bay consisting of an inset brick rectangle containing a smaller rounded arch window. The entire building was completed with a continuous cornice of local brick. The regularity of the building was notable and the detailing extremely crisp and well-crafted. Like most buildings of this decade the Brendlinger Block used the local reddish brick and a very light, almost white mortar. This mortar

Fillmore Block, 15th Street, between Blake and Market, 1868.

National Block, 1507 Blake, 1865.

Brendlinger Block, 1446 Blake, circa 1867
—partially demolished.

contrasted strongly with the brick, setting each individual brick off from the others and adding to the building's repetitive and classical character.

The only problem with the brick commercial architecture of Denver in the 1860's was that the buildings had no place on their facades for signs.[6] Various solutions to this problem were advanced in the city during that decade. The Brendlinger Block built brick signboards above the continuous cornice, on which the signs were painted. These large signs could be read from across the street, and smaller signs were painted above the windows or often in the windows to attract the attention of the stroller immediately adjacent to the building. Other establishments used signs which projected from the facade of the building like banners or flags. None of these solutions was entirely in keeping with the strength and sobriety of the architecture itself, but they did give the streets a little more variety and commercial life. As signs, they appear to have been much more restrained and tasteful than the signs which

15th Street, 1868.

were to adorn commercial buildings in the exuberant seventies.

Because a great deal of the population of Denver throughout the sixties and the seventies was transient, the construction of hotels, inexpensive rooming houses, and temporary apartments was an important portion of Denver real estate. The architecture of these buildings was little different from the architecture of the retail commercial structures. Hotels, saloons, and theaters were housed in brick boxes suitable to their often changing function. Theaters became saloons; houses became hotels; stores became theaters— the permutations and combinations were almost endless. A repetitive, classical, and multi-functional architecture catered to this unstable portion of the city's population.

Denver's institutional and residential architecture was not as severe and repetitious as the commercial architecture. Churches and houses did not have to be as densely packed and as flexible as commercial buildings. They were basically one-story structures with a simple gable facing the street. Their shape was similar to that of the log cabin, although they were more restrained, roomy, and attractive buildings. Denver did not legislate brick as the required domestic building material after the fire of 1863 as it had done for commercial architecture, and many of the smaller houses were constructed of sawed wood. Larger homes were brick, and as the decade proceeded some of the houses became two or two and one-half stories tall. Their massing and roof construction was more complex than that of commercial architecture, but they were elemental structures when compared to the domestic creations of the later seventies and eighties. Unornamented structures with simple roofs finished in small wooden shingles, they were often painted white. The porches had almost no bracket work, and the columns were plain hewn wood pillars with a rectangular base.[7] The Lawrence Street Church was one of the few buildings of that decade with any ostensible "style," and its gothic windows and pseudo-gothic pinnacles were an addendum to a basic brick rectangle with a basic brick tower. Any "style" or ornamental work which was added to these structures was clearly gratuitous and was generally wood. Ballustrades around porches and an occasional picket fence sufficed.

By 1867, Denver had emerged from its initial fears and frustrations. Already a strong territorial power, the little city could look forward to continued growth. Congress had passed the Continental Railroad Bill in 1862, and the construction program was beginning to move across the plains toward the center of the United States. Denver's future, while not secure, looked promising. Its only major competitor for the railroad was the infant Wyoming city of Cheyenne, and the struggle between these two small towns was of paramount importance in the history of the city in the later 1860's. When Cheyenne won out, many Denverites moved to Cheyenne in preparation for the coming of the railroad. Denver railroad builders were encouraged to build an extension to the transcontinental railway between Cheyenne and Denver by Territorial Governor Gilpin in 1869, in a speech which was an important indication of the change in Denver's self-image from isolated province to potential city, the center of the Rocky Mountain area.[8] Although Governor Gilpin's speech was in advance of his time, it was only slightly so. His remarks, which Smiley characterized quite correctly as "fervid, extravagant, and flowery," caught the imagination of the city, and the citizens of Denver talked of little else for weeks after the speech. Indeed, the extension was built to Denver, and it was completed in 1870. Denverites anticipated this event with a building campaign and a rush of hope for the future of their city.

View of Denver with Lawrence Street Methodist Church, circa 1864.

𝒯𝒽𝑒 Railroad City

Denver and the Nation
1870 – 1885

The year the first locomotive of the Denver Pacific Company steamed into the city was a year of indescribable excitement. Denver was, at last, plugged into the greatest communication network developed to that point. An attitude of excitement and nationalism began to characterize a city which only one or two years earlier had been dominated by fear, suspicion, and insularity, and numerous events solidified the region and placed it within the context of the United States of America. The railroad "arrived" on June 15, 1870, and this event gave 1870 a paramount importance in the history of the city.

As a small and isolated provincial town, Denver grew gradually during the 1860's to a population of around 4000. Its streets were ungraded and treacherous during rain and snow storms. There was little artificial illumination except tallow candles; there was no public water and no system of water pumping at all. The land around the city was parched and uninviting, and the great age of plains agriculture had not yet begun. All this changed within the year 1870. The Denver Gas and Electric Company was founded, the Denver City Water Company installed the city's first pumping station and set of pipes, and the city's streets were properly graded for the first time in its history. Settlement of the plains began; Greeley and Longmont were founded in 1870 and Colorado Springs in 1871. People began to flock to the burgeoning city of Denver, and, by 1872, it had doubled in population.

The trunk line from Cheyenne as well as the main track of the Kansas Pacific Railroad completed later in 1870 linked Denver with the east, the heartland of the United States in the nineteenth century. Mail service improved vastly, and periodicals, books, catalogs, yard goods, fashions, building supplies, and people began to flow into the city more steadily and at lower cost. Visitors came with increasing frequency, and families immigrated to the expansive and productive Territory of Colorado. The change in both the psyche and the physical condition of the city was immeasurable: the hotels were filled with new people and the theaters of Denver, some of which had closed in the last years of the 1860's, reopened, remodeled, and began a thriving business. Real estate sales shot upward and reached the million dollar mark for the first time in the city's history.[1] An era of growth began which was not really a boom in terms of the booms of the late seventies or the late eighties, but which was a highly optimistic period of expansion.

Denver began to show some signs of interest in questions of architectural style during the late 1860's. Several smallish commercial structures appeared with gothic arches on their lower level and segmental arches above. Others, like the Clark, Gruber and Company Bank and Mint (remodeled in the middle of the decade), sported a castellated tower at the center of the facade, and at least one building possessed a timid entrance arch above the center bay. These restrained, elegant uses of "style" were exceptional in the sober city of Denver during the 1860's, and they anticipated the more abandoned and unrestrained architecture of the railroad city. Gothic arches on a non-ecclesiastical building were common in American architecture of the middle nineteenth century, but they were revolutionary in Denver. Up to the end of the 1860's, Denver had maintained an unspoken system of stylistic appropriateness. Denverites gave their commercial buildings gravity by the use of the

*Architect Unknown/
1338 15th Street,
a fragment of the
only surviving building
from the 1860's with
gothic arches, circa 1869.*

Renaissance rounded arch; they gave their churches a "churchy" quality by the use of the gothic arch; and they gave their homes a "homey" quality by the addition of a balustraded front porch. The imagery was simple and was used consistently throughout the decade. The introduction of gothic arches on the Tappan Building, the first three-story building constructed in the city, seems pardonable within the system because it was used as a Masonic temple, but the appearance of the gothic arch on the totally commercial building around the corner of 15th and Market Streets from it indicates a dying of the concept of stylistic appropriateness in Denver. The imagery of the gothic church came into common use for commercial structures and, by 1871, appeared on a pumping house belonging to the Denver City Water Company.

The use of gothic arches on a commercial or a municipal building may seem insignificant to the modern reader, but it represented a considerable change in the attitude of Denverites toward architecture. No longer were buildings conceived as reductive brick masses to be ornamented as little as possible. In the late 1860's and especially after the arrival of the railroad in 1870, Denver buildings began to look like self-conscious *architecture;* they quoted and referred to the architecture of past civilizations with increasing frequency, and, after the arrival of the railroad, they began to participate in the architectural advances which were then revolutionizing continental and eastern American architecture.

Initially, the results were modest and tentative.

Gothic arches appeared only on brick cubes or rectangular solids. Buttresses, which were a prominent feature of the Lawrence Street Church, were small and simplified. American House, constructed in 1870 as Denver's first large hotel, was a three-story brick mass with small, simple windows and a regularized brick cornice in the manner of the sixties. The building's only departure from the western provincial mode was a train-imported wrought-iron balcony— an important indication of the changes in architecture brought by the Railroad Era.

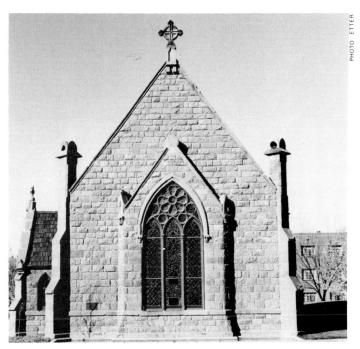

*Architect Unknown/Evans Chapel, presently sited at
Denver University, 1876.*

Pressed tin cornice and lintel detail, 1874—demolished.

Groff and Collins Building, circa 1888—demolished. This building is evidence of the continued use of the pressed tin cornice into the 1880's. Pressed tin cornices changed very little in style between 1870 and 1890. Denver architects like Edbrooke began to re-use brick and stone cornices by the middle of the 1880's with some consistency, and only relatively retardataire structures continued using the metal cornices in the later 1880's.

Granite Hotel, 1228 15th Street, cornice detail, 1883.

The use of metal in building construction was a phenomenon of the middle part of the century. The opening of the Crystal Palace at the Exposition of 1850 in England had sent architectural waves to every continent, and iron, which had been used since the end of the eighteenth century, soon became the most important and advanced building material of the nineteenth century. It was a symbol of modernity and strength to the inhabitants of every continent, and its arrival in Denver during the early years of the 1870's was made possible by the railroad. Even the train and the tracks on which it rode demonstrated the versatility of the metal. Its dark shiny surfaces emanated strength, and the passenger cars with their metallic parts and their shiny glass windows represented the first marriage of those two materials seen by the western American eye.

The most exciting quality of the newly available metal was the possibility of ornamental surface and design. After a decade of almost totally unornamented structures, Denverites related ornament with advanced civilization. The most skilled carpenter or brick layer could never produce a column as elaborate as a metal column; he could never make a filigree as detailed and exciting as the imported metal filigrees which began to come into the city. Brick cornices must have looked intolerably "home-made" in comparison to the tin and iron cornices which began to adorn the buildings of Denver in the 1870's. These architectural ornaments were composed of standardized elements, but had extremely active surfaces and were covered with incised lines and relief "carving." They were added to old buildings with brick cornices to "modernize" these buildings, and their widespread use during the early and middle seventies greatly increased the surface relief and the visual excitement of Denver's streets.

The dependence of Denver architecture on railroad-imported goods, mostly metal versions of composite cornices and Second Empire details, cannot be exaggerated. The architecture of the city became more confident and assertive as the 1870's wore on, eventually taking on the extreme ornamentation today known as "gingerbread."

Formal complexity and a pursuit of applique ornament are characteristic of the best and the most famous Colorado architecture of the 1870's. The fundamental structure of the buildings did not change significantly in the decade of the 1870's. Street buildings were still wooden boxes with brick facades, with iron at the front of the buildings to make them appear to be more advanced. Design was added by the application of pressed or molded metal ornament, which was often painted to look as if it were wood or stone.

A comparison of the Colorado Seminary of 1863-64 with the newer school buildings of Denver— the Arapahoe School of 1872 and the Stout Street School of 1873— makes clear the shift away from the relatively plain architecture of the 1860's to the ornamentation of the Railroad Era. The Colorado Seminary was a two-story brick box very similar in massing, size, and materials to the Stout Street School and the larger Arapahoe School. All three buildings were brick with some stone trim, and all three buildings had a central

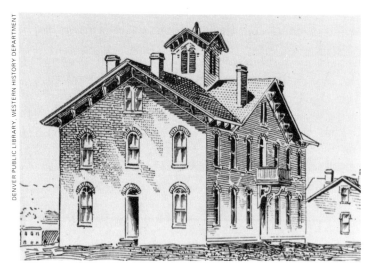

Architect Unknown/Colorado Seminary, 1863-64.

Stout Street School, 1873

cupola. The Seminary probably had no architect. The architect for the Stout Street School is unknown, and the architect for the Arapahoe School was a man named G.E. Randall who was not a Denverite. As architectural artifacts, the three buildings were virtually identical. The difference was clearly in the applied ornament. The cupolas of the Stout Street and the Arapahoe Schools were of considerable formal complexity, adorned by pressed metal columns, cornices, and roundels with their chimneys and sub-cupolas further decorated by wrought iron fences and weather vanes. The main cornice, which separated the roof from the brick wall in each of the three buildings, also demonstrates the difference in architectural style. In the Seminary building the slight overhang was allowed to float freely in plain splendor. In the Stout Street and Arapahoe Schools, metal cornices were held up with a double metal bracket, which became the major architectural ornament of the 1870's. It was used with restraint and intelligence in these early schools, but as the decade proceeded brackets proliferated to such an extent that their apparent structural function was lost. In many buildings of the late 1870's they no longer appeared to be holding up the cornice but rather weighing it down.

In 1873, the first *Denver Directory* appeared. This small publication is invaluable to the historian of early Denver culture; it described the city of Denver as it existed in the year 1872. Names and addresses of all the inhabitants were listed as well as their occupations, and the little book was made more useful by the introduction of a miniature "yellow pages" at the back of the book listing all commercial establishments of the city in

G.E. Randall (residence unknown)/Arapahoe School, 1872.

alphabetical order. A general introduction to the first two volumes of the directory presented statistics which included lists of prominent buildings and a table of the changes in tax assessment in certain parts of town. One surprising aspect of the 1873 *Denver Directory* is the listing of six firms (sometimes consisting of a single man) under "Architects and Superintend'ts."[2] Although none of these men had careers which are known to us today, they were undoubtedly the men who directed the expansion of the 1870's. The term architect was used then more broadly than it is today; there were no schools of architecture of the modern sort in mid-nineteenth century America and no system of accrediting architects until the 1890's. The profession consisted of men who were self-taught or who had gone through some sort of apprenticeship with another "architect" or builder. Of the terms "architect" and "superintendent," the latter is probably more applicable to the careers of these men. They were involved with a kind of architecture in which the builder constructed a conventional structure and the architect or superintendent advised on the details and the placement of ornament.[3] Architectural drawings from this period are rare in the west, and it is safe to assume that most architecture consisted of little more than on-site supervision. The early 1870's was still the age of the pattern book, and architecture came mostly from the studios of a very few men who worked for architectural magazines or who published books consisting of plans and elevations of the predominant building types. The local architect or construction supervisor interpreted the rather generalized "designs" which had been published in books and periodicals and oversaw the work from beginning to end.

The "style of the 1870's" was a provincial Second Empire, a cognate style which derived from French architecture of the great Parisian building campaign of Baron Huysman. Buildings like Visconti's addition to the Louvre of 1852-1857 and Garnier's Opera begun in 1864 became instantly famous and inspired a cognate mode of architectural planning which was practiced throughout Europe in the middle part of the century.[4]

The Second Empire style, characterized by mansard roofs, circular and round-arched windows, heavy cornices, and bilaterally symmetrical massing, was first used in the United States by James Renwick in his 1859 building for the Corcorran Gallery in Washington. This small, elegant building was a flattened version of the more elaborate Second Empire style in Europe, and it became well-known in America and the standard for a style which prevailed throughout the 1870's and into the 1880's. Second Empire buildings were constructed everywhere in America during the 1870's. The style was adapted to every kind of building with the possible exception of churches, for which it was thought too secular and exuberant to be used throughout the entire building. Its predominant character was institutional, and it was the primary style of court-houses, schools, and university buildings during the 1870's.

For Denverites, the Second Empire had few associations with specific European buildings. Rather, it stood for progress, modernism, and nationalism. The style adapted well to endless local variation, for it was based on a few relatively simple ornamental modules which could be combined in any of a number of compositions by the local building superintendent or "architect." It was used for domestic, commercial, and institutional architecture, with varying degrees of success. While its most prominent feature is the mansard roof, there are buildings constructed in Denver during the 1870's which lack the mansard roof and which remain Second Empire structures. The commercial structure at 1439 Larimer Street is the most notable of the surviving Second Empire structures which lack the mansard roof.

Architect Unknown/Crawford Building, 1439 Larimer Street, 1875.

Crawford Building, 1439 Larimer

The Crawford Building:
1439 Larimer Street

Built in 1875, its attenuated columns are made of cast iron as are the window caps and the cornice. The rest of the building is a wood-beamed, brick-edged box little different from the commercial structures of the 1860's. When the facade of this small Second Empire structure is compared with that of a typical commercial building of Denver in the previous decade, the old National Block (First National Bank, 1865) the difference is notable. The National Block had no central emphasis; its windows were identical and equidistant from one another; its cornice was flat, unprojecting, and eventless; and the arches on the ground floor exhibited a repetitive lateral rhythm. In contrast, the building at 1439 Larimer Street has light, delicate, asymmetrically placed columns on the first floor, which appear to push up rather than relate laterally to one another. The cornice is exuberant and heavy; its brackets are jammed close together to give a maximum surface activity, and it has no lateral continuity. The building is, in fact, grandly articulated in the center; instead of being composed of identical bricks, it fills the space of the facade with swooping curves which push together, interrupt each other, and engage in an almost voluptuous conversation about the center of the facade.

Centrality is the major characteristic of this facade. It does not attempt to relate to the buildings on either side of it either in size, scale, detailing, or composition. Decorative metal-work pushes toward the center of the building, drawing it away from its surroundings rather than tying it to the buildings on either side—1439 Larimer is trying to be as unique, as closed, as single, and as lavish as possible. Its detailing is overscaled and the window caps crowd each other out of the space. The desire is for thick, almost juicy ornament filled with

Iron column, Crawford Building.

Window detail, Crawford Building.

Pressed tin trim, Crawford Building.

interpenetrating curves. The style of the ornament is decidedly Second Empire and derives ultimately from the French Baroque. It was intended to give the streets of this provincial American town a grandeur and worldliness lacking in the more sober and timid architecture of Denver in the 1860's.

Even the brick regularity of the old National Block (the first permanent home of the First National Bank of Denver) gave way to Second Empire in the seventies, when an elegant mansard roof was added to provide a new third floor. The difference between the building as it stood in 1865 and after its addition indicates a change in architectural sensibilities in Denver. The addition of the roof united the building, pulling it together and giving it a centrality. Instead of wandering repetitively from arched window to arched window, the eye moved at once to the roof, which slanted slightly but significantly into the center of the building.[5]

This centrality of composition and the use of the new metal cornice brackets and window caps are the key features of the Second Empire style in Denver's commercial and institutional architecture. The mansard roof was often expensive and difficult to apply to a street-front commercial structure, and most Second Empire commercial structures did not have mansard roofs. There were also a number of institutional buildings of Second Empire character which lacked this characteristic feature. St. Mary's Academy of the early seventies, Wolfe Hall of 1873-1879, and the first building of Denver University built in 1879 are decidedly Second Empire in composition and in massing. They all lack the mansard roof which, as the decade of the 1870's continued, became less and less common in Denver's institutional architecture.

The old Guard Hall, completed in 1873, was perhaps the purest and most characteristic Second Empire building in the city. Its front facade displayed all the classic features of that style— pavilion massing, mansard roof, symmetry, and somewhat neo-Baroque detail. In addition, the building was expressive of the militarism and imperialism associated with the style. A photograph dating from the middle 1870's which shows the building as a backdrop for a military parade is further evidence of these associations.

Indeed, by the mid 1870's, American architects were adept at using mansard roofs, brackets, and columns, and the architecture of the Second Empire, while composed of standardized elements, did not possess a copy-book uniformity. Its use of mail-order ornamental motifs gave architects a great freedom from conventional constraint in their approach, a freedom which was to

STATE HISTORICAL SOCIETY OF COLORADO

Architect Unknown/National Block, 15th and Blake Streets, first two stories completed in 1865, roof added 1870's.

*Architect Unknown/Guard Hall,
1873–demolished.*

characterize the decade of Denver's eclecticism which will be discussed near the end of this book.[6] Brackets, cornices, towers, and fences were applied to brick boxes with great abandon and originality. Some Second Empire buildings in Denver were almost totally unornamented and others were characterized by a profusion of ornament. In short, the style was extremely flexible. It could be used on a wide variety of buildings in a wide variety of ways without becoming unrecognizable or just bad. Its imagistic association with imperialistic Europe must have seemed appropriate to the new settlers of the American west, settlers whose ideas were charged with the then common notions of manifest destiny and who imagined themselves to be the conquerers of a truly uncivilized land. Its connection with the railroad reinforced its modernity and its industrial quality. It had the advantages of association with power in both a political and a literal sense.

Larimer Street, circa 1880.

When examined as a whole, Denver's homes of the 1870's have a remarkable consistency regardless of their "style." The bracketed mode, the Italian villa type, and Second Empire vied for dominance in Denver's homes of that decade, but the buildings which exhibit one or the other of these "styles" were often more similar than different. The H.P. Hill mansion, formerly at 14th and Welton Streets, was decidedly Second Empire in its detailing, but seemed remarkably similar to the Byers house, presently at 13th and Bannock, which has very few Second Empire features. Both buildings were brick boxes with stepped massing restrained by the dominat-ing cornice or mansard roof; both buildings used neo-classical cornices and wrought iron roof detail, and both buildings had remarkably similar plans. This homogeneity of Denver's domestic architecture was quite marked in the early and middle 1870's. By the end of that decade and certainly by the beginning of the 1880's, it began to break down, and the restrained variety of styles characteristic of the 1870's gave way to a newer, wilder, and more eclectic architecture.

The Second Empire began a slow and rather painless death later in the 1870's and continued feebly into the 1880's. The early commercial structures of Roeschlaub

Architect Unknown/Third Byers house (the Evans house), 1310 Bannock, circa 1878.

and Edbrooke, built in the late seventies and early eighties, show a picturesque and asymmetrical massing as well as a use of detail derived fundamentally from England. The Philadelphia Exposition of 1876 brought advanced English architecture to the United States, and American architects wasted little time in switching their allegiance from Second Empire to High Victorian. The railroad, which early in the 1870's had brought the Second Empire style to the city of Denver, brought a great many other influences as well. Denver buildings became decidedly more confused, experimental, and eclectic. No longer did construction superintendents supervise the locals from national pattern books. The new architects of Denver, although influenced by eastern and midwestern architecture to a great extent, were not pattern book designers. Around 1880, after the completion of the Tabor Block and the Tabor Grand Opera House, and certainly by the middle of that decade, Denver had changed again from the Railroad City to the Architect's City. It was a city built in a boom, but built intelligently and beautifully.

Late Second Empire house, architect unknown, owner unknown, location unknown. This house probably dates from the middle of the 1880's and is an example of Second Empire details grafted to the plan and massing of a Queen Anne house.

Architect Unknown/First building of Denver University, 1879-80–demolished. Typical of the cognate mode or style which dominated Denver architecture of the 1870's.

The Architects' City

The Rise of Regional Architecture in Denver
1879–1893

Frustratingly little documentary evidence survives to describe Denver's earliest architects. The *Denver Directory,* a coldly organized source, was not designed for the biographical historian, and the *Western Architect and Building News,* in spite of its completeness and its excellence, was published for only two years. It is difficult to date precisely the arrival of an architect to the city of Denver. American architects, especially provincial American architects, were often untrained and certainly unaccredited in the 1870's. Their roles in the architectural process were limited primarily to construction supervision, and the listing of six architectural firms in the first issue of the *Denver Directory,* issued in 1873, must be viewed with some

reservation. Robert Roeschlaub, who was the city's first great architect, arrived in 1873, and clearly brought with him a knowledge of the actual design process. His drawings, most of which date from the 1880's, are skillful and attractive, indicative of an architect with more than a pattern book idea of the process of design. His buildings from the seventies must be seen in terms of the predominant Second Empire style then fashionable throughout the United States, but they evidence an unusual restlessness within the conventions of that style. Roeschlaub, like Edbrooke, created buildings which stood out among the artful confections of the Second Empire.

The concentration of architects in Denver in the early years of the seventies can probably be explained by the railroad, which was the west's greatest cultural messenger in the nineteenth century. As the growth of the middle seventies tapered, the number of architects also declined. Only Roeschlaub, in his office at the corner of 15th and Larimer, survived the decade unscathed, with no change of address, no brief disappearance, no change of partner. The architects of the 1870's, with the single exception of Roeschlaub, seem to have been highly mobile, sent around the region to build in the smaller mining towns of Colorado or in the incipient agricultural villages of the plains.

Denver, in spite of its growth, was not a large city in the 1870's. It was the center of a region, the state capital, but it was not really the cosmopolitan center envisioned by Gilpin in 1869. Denver's future as a great urban power was not really established until 1879, when H.A.W. Tabor decided to build in Denver and went to Chicago, at that time the greatest city in the west, to find his architect. His choice was the Edbrooke brothers. They had no advantage over the local architects as far as training went, but Frank, the younger of the two, did have incredible ambition, brains, and social acumen. He single-handedly turned Denver into an architects' city, and his buildings were Denver's first buildings which were up to national par.

Frank Edbrooke's arrival in 1879 was an auspicious arrival indeed, and Tabor's willingness to spend his millions on buildings gave a much-needed boost to Denver's construction business. The Tabor Block and the Tabor Grand Opera House changed the scale of Denver's downtown dramatically after their completion in 1881, and they gave a new standard of size, luxury, and architectural excellence which guided the boom of the eighties and influenced other builders to have their structures designed rather than merely built. The *Denver Directory* of 1879 listed three architects, Anthony, Nichols, and Roeschlaub, none of whom could afford to advertise as they had in earlier years. The 1880 directory listed ten architects, some of whom remained in Denver for many years, and the 1881 edition listed

19 architects, a majority of whom paid extra for large-letter ads. By 1883 the number of architects in the city numbered 40— and Denver had clearly become the architects' city.

Beginning in the 1880's, Denver's buildings were designed and built almost exclusively by her own architects. It has long been fashionable to assume that buildings in the nineteenth century were "made up" by their owners, copied from pattern books, or simply built with little if any pre-existing plan. In the case of Denver's growth in the 1880's and later, this assumption is totally untrue. By the late nineteenth century Denver had a large and self-conscious body of architects, architects who were able draftsmen, sophisticated designers, and in many cases experienced builders. Their internal relations were at times characterized by fierce competition and, occasionally, personal rivalry, but as a group they were professionals, and in that capacity they designed and built the nineteenth century city of Denver.

Denver and The Nation

By the 1880's the architectural profession in America was characterized by an increasing self-consciousness. Architectural training in universities was instituted in the later 1870's, and American architects began a period of intense creation. From California to the east coast architects began to voice discontent about the "second-rate" quality of American architecture— about the fact that there was nothing truly "American" about the architecture designed and built in this country. The one hundredth anniversary of the United States was designed for national reflection upon America's achievement, and the Philadelphia Exposition of that year, with its pavilions from England and Japan, demonstrated to many Americans that their civilization was architecturally out-of-date. The decade which followed the exposition was in many ways the most important decade in the history of American architecture. The career of H.H. Richardson matured and became publicly known; the metal technology of the 1870's was developed to a new high level; the commercial architecture of Chicago, among the greatest American architecture of any time, underwent its first phase of development; and the shingle style was revolutionizing domestic architecture on the east coast. In the decade which followed, the new cities of the Rocky Mountains and the far west experienced unparalleled building booms, and there were undoubtedly more buildings constructed in the west in the 1880's than in all previous decades of the

I. Hodgson/The McMurtrie house. Drawing by the architect, published in the Western Architect and Building News. *1890–demolished.*

William Cowe/Competition drawing of a wayside inn, Denver Architectural Sketch Club, published in the Western Architect and Building News.

nineteenth century combined. While the hazards of boom time are obvious— sloppy design and careless construction due to hasty planning— the advantages were also great. Men of visionary stature and imagination were given an unbelievable opportunity to realize their dreams, and paper architecture, which previous to the nineteenth century had been the sole medium of many great architects, materialized into buildings at a greater rate than ever before.

Denver thought of herself in that period as a city.[1] Denverites were not concerned with building a nice little town nestled at the foot of the Rockies. Rather, they wanted to build one of the great cities in the history of civilization, and do it within the decade. These dreams, in spite of their silliness and pretension, were materialized with surprising completeness. The boom of the latter 1880's was perhaps the greatest construction boom in the history of Denver, rivaling in scope, quality, and complexity the building boom of the late sixties and early seventies in the twentieth century. New citizens came from around the country and around the world, and magazines and catalogs poured into Denver along with the latest designs and technological advancements. Denverites of the nineteenth century, like Denverites today, wore the same clothes, read the same books and magazines, lived in the same kind of houses, rode the same tramways, and essentially lead the same lives as people from Minneapolis, Chicago, Cincinnati, Cleveland, New York, and Boston.

Franklin Kidder/Christ Methodist Episcopal Church, 1889. Drawing by the architect published in the Western Architect and Building News.

Architects and their clients lived in a truly national milieu, no longer afraid of the Indians, the wilds of the mountains, and the lawless ruffians who had haunted the populace of Denver in the 1860's. The railroad penetrated nearly every corner of the state. The mountains were characterized in the 1880's and 1890's as pleasure gardens, as tamed nature, as wilds made habitable by modern man— W.H. Jackson's photographs show men in bowler hats and ladies in long dresses lounging by mountain lakes, standing atop pinnacles, and climbing adventurously up cliffs. The train, that metallic marvel which looks so dated to twentieth century eyes, was a symbol of modernity and mastery over the Rocky Mountains.

Stone, brought from local quarries, began to replace the local brick as the most popular and prestigious building material. If a builder could afford it, he finished his building in large blocks of heavily rusticated stone, intended to convey visually superhuman strength and solidity.[2] As a new regional strength joined with an increasing national awareness among provincial Americans, architects of the west were provided with an ideal situation in which to invent and expand American architecture. The newness, vastness, and beauty of the west were considered tamed at last, and western

Americans began to build cities which they saw as rivaling the cities of Europe and the ancient world.

The expansion of American culture in the 1880's produced an expansion of architectural vocabulary. Pattern books were a thing of the past, and a national architectural press was expanding dramatically in scope and visual interest. The *American Architect and Building News,* the country's leading national journal, increased in size, circulation, and quality of illustration in the 1880's. Regional magazines were founded with rapidity and success, and the *Inland Architect and Building News* of Chicago, the *Northwestern Architect and Building Budget* from Minneapolis, and the *Architectural Era* from Syracuse were the major publications subscribed to by Denver architects. These magazines were filled with linocuts, floorplans, drawings, lists, lectures, and newsletter articles. They were almost always well illustrated, well designed, expensive and intelligent. Each of the local magazines had a national subscription, and the architects of one region were very familiar with the work of their colleagues across the nation. None of the smaller regions within the United States experienced any crises of confidence; none of them felt subservient or inferior to the older cities of the east coast. Their relationships were closer in many

Miller and Janisch/Drawing of a projected apartment building published in the Western Architect and Building News.

John Spencer/Competition drawing of a city front, competition of the Denver Architectural Sketch Club, published in the Western Architect and Building News.

ways than they are today, and the architects of Denver learned a great deal from the architects of Minneapolis and Syracuse.

Denver architects relied on the national and regional periodicals throughout the early part of the 1880's. The building boom which began in 1880 reached a high in 1883. The slight recession which followed became by 1885 a downright slump, and the number of architects in Denver dropped from 40 in 1883 to about 20 in 1885, only to increase again in 1888. Architects came to Denver from the east coast, from Europe, and from the western or mid-western United States. They came because Denver was a boom town, because it was in the new and adventurous west, and because the mines stabilized the economy of the region, at least until the great silver crash of 1893. The careers of these men were characterized by a competitive spirit and a desire to out-build and out-design the other local members of the profession. Many buildings are known to have been designed in competition by two or three local architects, only one of whom got the job. This practice, common as it is today, was then even more widespread and much less gentlemanly. Architects upstaged each other at presentations and pitted their skills against one another in frequent drafting contests as the 1880's wore on. Business was plentiful, but the number of choice jobs was limited. Each architect wanted his share of the large commercial buildings, the schools, and the churches with substantial budgets. The taller a building, the greater its prestige, and expensive buildings were often given very favorable treatment in the popular press. Architecture was a source of pride for all the local

inhabitants of the burgeoning western cities, and a great many publications devoted to Denver's fine homes and buildings appeared during that decade.

Although Denver architects were powerful and interesting throughout the 1880's, they have eluded the historian of architecture with remarkable facility. Buildings constructed between 1880 and 1888 are difficult to attribute because almost no documents exist; for some reason, architects were simply not mentioned often in nineteenth century accounts of buildings. The information given about a building might include its cost, its size, the various contractors who put in the glass, stone or plumbing, the owner, the materials, and a testimony to its modernity, but the architect was almost never mentioned by name. The building was simply described as being from the best class of work in the city, whatever that meant.

In spite of the lack of mention by name in nineteenth century architectural literature, architects were treated as professionals.[3] It was important for a local merchant to have his house and his store designed by an architect, and many men, like M. Kittredge, were notable architectural patrons whose buildings were designed by several good local architects. This kind of patronage was not uncommon among the rich merchants and miners of Denver, although most of the patrons were more consistent in their choice of one architect.

Denver Buildings by National Architects

Some Denverites, in their desire to be truly fashionable, imported architects from other American cities to design their buildings. This practice was far less common than has been supposed, but it gave Denver architects buildings of national stature to emulate or compete with. The Boston firm of Andrews, Jacques, and Rantoul designed two large and important commercial structures in Denver, the Boston Block in 1889 and the Equitable Building in 1890. Both buildings are impressive structures, but they have been over-evaluated by Denverites ever since their construction.

The Boston Block is a good building, but it is not an advanced skyscraper for its date. It seems to be most clearly describable as a combination of Richardsonian architecture, then fashionable in Denver and throughout the nation, and the more Italianate Renaissance revival which was popularized in the later eighties by Stanford White. The facade of the Boston Block relates most obviously to the Renaissance palazzo, but the color of the stone and the repetitive grandeur of the arches as well as the rough, even primitive cornice seem more akin to Richardson's Marshall Field Warehouse in Chicago. The building as it stands today has lost its cornice, the balcony which adorned the 17th Street facade, and most of the architectural ornament, and it looks more austere and more Richardsonian than it did in the 1890's.

The Equitable Building is more ostensibly Renaissance in its style. It makes few references to Richardson and seems to be retardataire in its complex massing and surface patterning. Both buildings were among Denver's most conspicuous commercial structures in the nineteenth century. But although they were impressive and exerted some influence on the architects of Denver they are decidedly weaker than the commercial structures of Frank E. Edbrooke in their complex and unresolved layering and in their almost pompous imagery of the palazzo.

Ironically, the buildings constructed in Denver by the firm of Andrews, Jacques, and Rantoul probably added to the self-confidence of Denver's own architects. It was easy to see that the commercial structures of Edbrooke were as large, as expensive, and as good as the work of these enlightened and probably well-trained easterners. Denverites began to realize with increasing pride that their own architects were as good as almost any architect from any other city. When wealthy Denverites began to build very large office structures in the later 1880's and early 1890's, they chose Denver architects almost exclusively, and Denver differed sharply from San Francisco, Kansas City and Omaha in that it had no buildings by prominent architects from New York or Chicago. Of the large structures built in Denver from the 1880's until well into the twentieth century, only three were designed by firms from outside Denver. Denverites, it seems, had a trust in their own architects which almost never wavered, and which proved extremely beneficial for the building boom. Local architects knew

Andrews, Jacques and Rantoul (Denver and Boston)/
The Boston Block, 17th and Champa Streets, 1889.

Andrews, Jacques and Rantoul (Denver and Boston)/
The Equitable Building, 17th and Stout Streets, 1890.

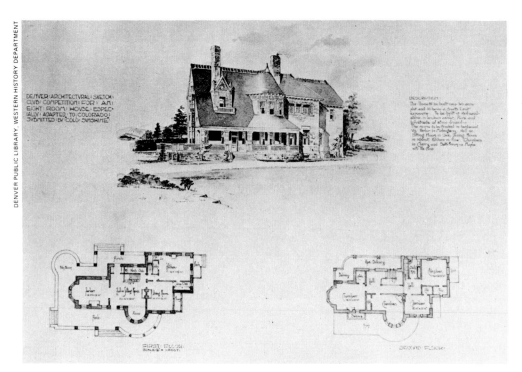

*Anonymous entry in the competition
for an eight room house especially
adapted to Colorado,
Denver Architectural Sketch Club,
published in the*
Western Architect and Building News.

the local construction firms, the local building materials, and, most important, the local clients. They could respond more interestingly and more intelligently to the city's tastes and desires because they lived with and experienced those tastes and desires.

The Western Architect and Building News

The most important reason for the architectural consciousness of the later eighties and for the increasingly high quality of local architecture was the founding in 1889 of Denver's own architectural magazine, the *Western Architect and Building News.* The magazine guided, shaped, and, in a sense, controlled the building boom. It brought Denver architects from their hopeless, competitive morass of the middle 1880's into a more serene competition. It pushed for civic improvements with a persistence lacking in modern architectural journalism. It was responsible for the organization of Denver architects and for the education of the Denver public which led to their becoming one of the most enlightened groups of architectural patrons in the west.

The magazine was founded by a well-educated, energetic, and responsible man named J.B. Dorman.[4] Dorman tried to begin the magazine early in 1888. He was somewhat discouraged by the lack of support from both the architectural and the business communities, a lack of support which he described a year later in the first issue of the magazine.

"It was thought that Denver was not quite ready for a monthly publication of such an ambitious nature as this; the field seemed narrow, and while many spoke encouragingly of the enterprise, many more were of the opinion that Denver and the surrounding country could not afford sufficient support."[5]

By early in 1889, conditions had changed markedly. The building boom was in full swing, the mines were maintaining a steady production, and the agricultural communities were beginning construction campaigns. The population of the city was rising; house construction was brisker than it had ever been; the retail market was decidedly up. Both businesses and architects, flushed with new success, supported the infant publication, and its first issue was impressive enough to encourage further support. Dorman gave an effulgent account of the aims and the success of the publication in its first issue.

"The illustrations will show the style and solidity of our buildings, and will demonstrate more plainly than words the wonderful progress of Denver in the last ten years. To accomplish this object in a quiet and truthful manner with no great flourish of trumpets, is the aim of its publishers. No journal ever started in Colorado has had more flattering prospects, and certainly none has ever met with readier support."[6]

The first issue of the *Western Architect and Building News* must have seemed a marvel to Denver readers. The magazine was large, impressively designed, and well illustrated. It contained advertisements from all the prominent Denver architectural firms as well as from a few which were not so prominent. Its prose was clear, concise, and pointed. It was infused with a pride both civic and regional, and its articles were varied and, more important, short. Illustrations were supremely well chosen. The Denver Club was prominently featured with a rendering of its exterior and architect drawings of its furniture. Dorman was, no doubt, appealing for support from Denver's wealthy and influential businessmen who belonged to the club. The Kittredge building was

*Morris Stuckert/Watercolor of the
J. Beaumont house, projected for Pueblo,
Colorado, published in the* Western Architect
and Building News.

pictured as rendered by its architect Morris Stuckert, and the recently completed Denver Public High School by Roeschlaub appealed to Denver's immediate past. The Kittredge building and the Denver Club were both new, built of local rusticated stone and standing proudly in the newly developed uptown. Roeschlaub's building was older, more official and more serene. It related to Denver's civic side, her schools and institutions which were being built throughout the 1880's. This first issue accented the strength, scale, and richness of native Denver architecture. It featured buildings in the architect's own drawings, a technique which was to become a hallmark of the magazine. It was the first publication in the history of Denver which discussed architects by name, which pointed with pride to local engineers and contractors, which was both civic and regional in its scope, and which considered Denver architecture as important architecture. Dorman quoted A.E. Burkhardt, a merchant from Cincinnati, who wrote an article about the west in the *Cincinnati Times Star* of April 10, 1889.

"Originality and perfection in architecture are no longer looked for among the old fogies of the East. They are now all found in the active, energetic, and punching West."[7]

The *Western Architect and Building News* proved to be more than a local periodical during the two years of its publication. It featured architectural renderings from Cincinatti, photographs of buildings from Galveston and Salt Lake City, notes from throughout the state, reprints of lectures given in Cleveland or Cincinnati, and many other tidbits which had little to do with Denver.

The magazine was extremely varied in its selection of illustrations and the approach used by its authors. One correspondent of the epicurean school of architectural criticism, for example, referred to the Mays house as "comfortable and tasty."[8] Others were more interested in problems of structure and construction costs. The magazine had a long series of articles, letters, more articles, and then more letters on the subject of the proper paving material for Denver streets. Some writers, like the businessman Creswell, claimed that hard stone should be used for the downtown streets because commerce was increased immeasurably in the midst of a busy, clattering noise; others favored the less noisy surface of asphalt. The smaller articles in the magazine were truly nineteenth century in their scope and slant. One piece told the reader how to plant trees, another how to get rid of mosquitos, and yet another how to manufacture Roman bricks. Repeatedly there were articles on materials— artificial stones, metals, and asphalt. The softness of new mortars was decried and the virtues of the old mortar were extolled.

As far as style and taste in architecture, the magazine apparently had no bias. Buildings which derived from the Chicago school of commercial architecture were published as often as houses in the late Queen Anne, eclectic mode. Simplicity and complexity vied for attention on adjacent pages. Houses were not favored over institutional or commercial buildings, and buildings for middle-class patrons were more numerous than extravagant buildings designed for the rich. Although the magazine often mentioned the high quality of Denver's homes, it shied away from depicting the most

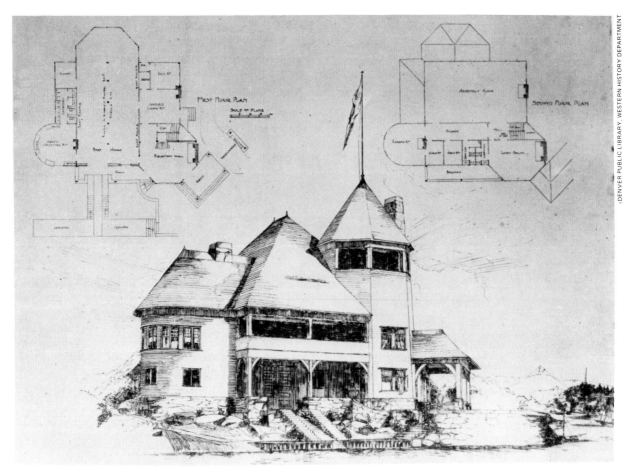

John J. Huddart/Competition drawing of a boathouse, Denver Architectural Sketch Club, published in the Western Architect and Building News.

John J. Huddart/Competition drawing of a boathouse, Denver Architectural Sketch Club, published in the Western Architect and Building News.

expensive and the largest houses in the city. It chose instead to publicize buildings which many people could afford to emulate.

Perhaps the greatest achievement of the *Western Architect and Building News* was its role in unifying and organizing the architectural community in the city. Dorman was tireless in his attempts to encourage communication among the architects in the city and to provide a forum in which the best of their work, regardless of its style, could be made public. The magazine, thanks undoubtedly to its editor, had a national circulation. It was sent to architects and libraries all over the country and to every small-town newspaper in Colorado and Utah. Dorman seems to have been somewhat biased against Kansas, Nebraska, and Wyoming; his emphasis was on the states which were further west and further south than Colorado. He ran a series of articles, radical for the time, on the architecture of old New Mexico, but the articles had no measurable effect on Denver architecture during the period of the magazine's publication. His first issue made a plea for the formation of a Denver architectural sketch club and offered the magazine's offices as a meeting place for any night of the week. The next issue of the magazine announced the formation of the society and printed its minutes, and, subsequent issues printed its drawings. Curiously, the architects who comprised the membership of the Denver Architectural Sketch Club were among the least prominent in the city. Many

of the names are unfamiliar and, after a perusal of the *Denver Directory,* turn out to have been draftsmen for the more important architects whose names became associated with the city's buildings. Denver seems to have had a very active and very aesthetically conscious population of drafters. These men may well have been the chief designers of the firms to which their names are attached. Their designs are often very impressive, if small-scale, and they must have had an important role in the design process in many of the city's most notable offices.[9]

Architecture, to Dorman, was the most democratic, the most pervasive, and the most important of the arts. It touched the life of every man regardless of his stature or wealth, and Dorman wanted everyone to become involved in the great enterprise of building the west. The magazine was notable for the attention which it paid to specific architects, and was in addition the official organ for the Colorado Society of Engineers. Dorman wanted businessmen to become active in architectural matters and to exert some enlightened and responsible leadership in the city. The *Western Architect and Building News* was, in short, a rudder guiding the course of the building boom. It provided a forum for all kinds of writers, politicians, architects, and thinkers. Dorman was a man who rarely avoided taking a strong position on a particular matter, but he was also a very fair man. Both of Denver's construction scandals of the nineteenth century, one involving a chimney which

T.A. Green/Competition drawing of a suburban club house, Denver Architectural Sketch Club, published in the Western Architect and Building News.

collapsed in 1889 at Roeschlaub's Ebert School and the other which centered on the strength of the piers at the base of Stuckert's Kittredge building, were covered in full by the *Western Architect and Building News.* All the documents concerning the architects were printed, no matter how repetitive and tedious they were, and in both cases the architects' names were cleared. Dorman was a tireless fighter for quality environment and for good architecture. He was interested, as were all late nineteenth century architectural thinkers and theorists, in buildings as monuments which may stand forever and which must function properly. He was greatly concerned with the problems of adequate ventilation and evidenced a knowledge of the pioneering work of Florence Nightingale in hospital design. His prose was clear and direct, unlike Ruskin whom he seems to have admired greatly. He kept architects abreast of each other's work with monthly listing of buildings from all over Colorado and often Utah. He sent writers throughout the region to photograph and report on architectural expansion in the south and the southwest. He had, in short, a formidable mind and a formidable constitution. Like many activists of the late nineteenth century, he was not afraid to think big and act big and to do as many things at once as he could possibly do. His effect on Denver was immeasurable. The city would have been built without him, but it would not have been built as well.

Dorman's Denver

Denver responded with an unusual fervor to Dorman's magazine and Dorman's pleas for decent architecture. After the magazine's demise for lack of funds in August of 1891, its effects on the city lived on. Thomas Tonge, the formidable local publicist and historian, wrote pamphlets about the charms and beauty of Denver which had a national circulation, and the Union Pacific Railroad began national publication of W.H. Jackson's photographs of the city and its new buildings. A massive photographic record of Denver developed, showing her buildings, her interiors, her parks, her streets, her institutions, her amusements, and her people.[10] Guidebooks to the city began to appear, and Denver's reputation as a city of beautiful homes, parks, and institutions took on national proportions.

Denver architects made their most important attempt at organization and accreditation only four months after the *Western Architect and Building News* ceased publication. The Dorman-initiated organization called the Colorado Association of Architects met in December of 1891 and decided to apply for membership as a chapter of the American Institute of Architects.[11] The application was made after a unanimous vote, and membership in the national organization was received by the association four months later. The architects of Denver

Miller and Janisch/Drawing of a projected house published in the Western Architect and Building News.

now had a nationally accredited organization with monthly meetings. The officers of this group included Robert Roeschlaub, E.R. Rice, H.W. Baerresen, and Frank E. Edbrooke, and the membership included every prominent architect in the city. There were no resignations in the first several years, and members attended meetings with surprising regularity. This organization, with its regular meetings and its aggregate power, was the fulfilment of Dormer's dreams and stands as the final proof that Denver was an architects' city. Its thirty-one members, all but one of whom were Denver architects, banded together to work on a new lien law and to improve the city's building ordinance. They concerned themselves not only with the design of beautiful and expensive buildings. They took collective and professional responsibility for the shape of the entire city of Denver.

Denver was built almost exclusively in the six years between 1888 and 1893. Its buildings from that period are its most confident, its most attractive, and its most important. Many of Denver's present institutional buildings date from that period— Denver University, Loretto Heights, Colorado Women's College, St. Joseph's Hospital, St. Luke's Hospital, National Jewish Hospital, St. Anthony's Hospital, Central Presbyterian Church, Christ Methodist Church, Asbury Methodist Church, St. Mark's Church, and many Denver Public Schools. As the mines reached their peak of production and Colorado gained national prominence for its climate and its other natural resources, thousands of people began the migration to Denver which resulted in the boom of the later eighties and early nineties. When an electric street car system

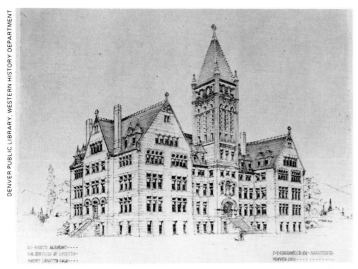

Frank E. Edbrooke/Drawing for the St. Mary's Academy for the Sisters of Loretto, 1890, published in the Western Architect and Building News.

installed in 1885 failed due to the extreme cost of the venture, it was superceded in the late eighties by the successful construction of a cable car system. Fares were reasonable, and the system, as it was in operation by the early nineties, made inner city travel very easy and inexpensive. Various civic advantages of Denver attracted a vast number of easterners to the city, and its climate and altitude drew many who suffered from tuberculosis and other respiratory ailments. Denver was probably the most health-conscious city in the United States in the nineteenth century. It was filled with sanitoriums, hospitals, and rest homes. Its homes were constructed with sleeping porches for the cure of tuberculosis, and ventilation became one of the major concerns in the construction of many public and commercial buildings in the city. The age of irresponsibility, lawlessness, and insularity was an historical age to Denverites of the late eighties. The children and the grandchildren of the pioneers were vastly out-numbered by Denver's new citizens. Oscar Wilde remarked in 1883 on his visit to Denver that he had never before experienced a city in which none of its citizens had been born. This historical thinness was, perhaps, the major enemy of Denverites in the decade from 1883-1893. Denver's reliance on stone and brick as major building materials must be seen in light of a desire to build a solid, stable, and lasting city, a city which looked permanent and complete. Denverites hired architects and builders to design and construct a noble city to be as different as possible from the little town which began in 1858 and its successor, the Railroad City with its mail-order culture.

There were three major architects in nineteenth century Denver: Frank E. Edbrooke, William Lang, and Robert Roeschlaub. Edbrooke and Roeschlaub established careers which were long and profitable, and are fairly well documented. Lang is more elusive, an architect who came to Denver in 1886 and left the city after the great crash of 1893 and about whom little is known. His buildings, which exemplified the late eclectic mode in Denver, attest to his greatness as the most able domestic designer in the city of Denver in the nineteenth century.

These three architects stand without question as the strongest architects of the city during their lives—architects whose works were constantly mimicked, copied, and challenged by their lesser contemporaries.

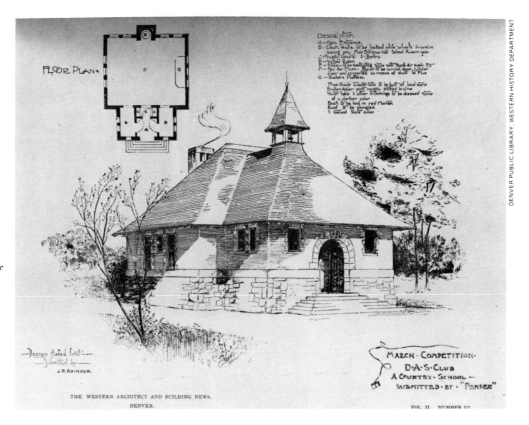

J.R. Rainbow/Competition drawing of a country schoolhouse, Denver Architectural Sketch Club, published in the Western Architect and Building News.

The Major Architects

Frank E. Edbrooke

The Commercial Architect

Frank E. Edbrooke (1840-1918) was almost single-handedly responsible for the architectural maturity of Denver's downtown in the late 1880's and 1890's. A master of street architecture, he designed office blocks, street buildings and warehouses which transformed a commercial area of rather finicky Second Empire buildings into a grand, large-scaled, and beautifully articulated grid. His facades and corner buildings look very advanced when compared to the well-known masterpieces of so-called skyscraper architecture by prominent Chicago firms such as Adler and Sullivan or Burnham and Root. An illustrated list of his complete works indicates a commercial success and importance almost as great as that of the larger Chicago, New York, and Minneapolis firms, and the best of his work— the Brown Hotel, the California Building, the

People's National Savings Bank, the Central Presbyterian Church, the Warren residence, and the Club Building— equals and in some cases surpasses the work of his more famous contemporaries. The fact that he is totally ignored by modern historians of nineteenth century commercial architecture in America is indicative of the regional bias which has characterized that scholarship for several generations.

The Tabor Buildings: Denver in 1879

After a brief career as a railroad architect, Frank E. Edbrooke came to Denver in 1879 to supervise construction of the Tabor Block on Larimer at 16th Street and stayed until his death in 1918.[1] He shared design responsibility for the Opera House and the Tabor Block with his brother, W.J. Edbrooke, and since none of Frank Edbrooke's earlier hotels survive in documented form it is impossible to tell which brother did what in the Tabor buildings. The fact that Frank was sent to the site suggests that he was more versed in construction supervision.[2] Both Tabor buildings possessed an exuberance and activity characteristic of their client and were certainly the most sumptuous buildings designed by the Edbrooke brothers to that date. Stylistically Second Empire, they were extremely important in the history of Denver urbanism because of their size and social importance in the then-small town of Denver. The Opera House and the Tabor Block were thought of as Denver's first truly civilized buildings. Their rather freely adapted Second Empire classicism combined happily with the harder and sharper details of the High Victorian street building with its architectural gadgetry— brackets, panels, pinnacles, and almost flattened segmental arches.

The Tabor Block was the more active of the two. Its complex light-gray limestone surface was intended to evoke H.A.W. Tabor's reputed skill as a stone mason, and there are many (probably apocryphal) stories of the millionaire himself cutting and laying stones with gusto alongside the workmen. The building's predominant verticality was held in check by the pair of strong cornices which appeared to be supported both by the pilasters and by the brackets which also supported the window slabs. The tension between vertical and horizontal, square-topped and segmentally arched windows, symmetry and asymmetry, structure and the appearance of structure, incision and relief all were manifest in the facade of the building and prefigured the aesthetic of tension and contradiction which continued to play a large role in Denver architecture until 1893. The building was brash, reticulated, and problematic, certainly belonging to the late Second Empire phase of American urban design. It retained a reasonably correct classicism in the cornice while flagrantly violating the classical orders, either Roman or Greek, in the pilasters

Frank E. Edbrooke (?)/Tabor Block, 1879-80–demolished.

Frank E. Edbrooke (?)/Tabor Block, 16th and Larimer Streets.

and incised designs. Although the beveled corner rarely appears in Edbrooke's later work, many other elements such as the grouping of several floors into one composition (with the large-scale pilasters) and the partially articulated center entrance on the long facade reappeared many times in his later office buildings.

The Tabor Block, well received after its completion in 1880, continued to house architects' offices into the nineties, but the Tabor Grand Opera House left a more decisive mark on Denver. This building, huge by Denver standards and costly as well ($750,000), has received so many conflicting style names in its history that its eclecticism has been wildly exaggerated. Eugene Field innocently started the whole process in 1881 when he

described the building as "modified Egyptian moresque."[3] Since then, the building has been called everything from Renaissance to Romanesque, and neither seems particularly appropriate. Actually, the building as it was originally designed (the quasi-mansard roof was straightened in later years for reasons of expansion) had both Second Empire and High Victorian gothic features. The massing of the building may have been derived from the palace type exemplified in Visconti's 1852-57 addition to the Louvre. This massing— a long facade interrupted by a central entrance tower and two corner towers— was well-known in American architecture of the 1870's. Its use in the prestigious Tabor Opera House was, however, modified considerably by the inequality of tower height and the resulting lack of symmetry. The English "picturesque" silhouette combined with the wrought iron detail, the lack of any clearly defined mansard roof, and the use of somewhat gothic segmental arches to give the building a decidedly High Victorian character. It seems to have more to do with the Law Courts Competition of 1869 and the other buildings which came out of England's Houses of Parliament than it does with the symmetrical and often lumpy classicism of the American Second Empire style itself. Whatever its style, the Tabor Grand Opera House became a pattern for large-scale Denver architecture throughout the early 1880's, influencing the design of such buildings as the Windsor Hotel, the Markham Hotel, and, of all buildings, the First Baptist Church, which was designed by Edbrooke in 1883.

Frank E. Edbrooke (?)/Tabor Grand Opera House, 1879-80. —demolished.

Frank E. Edbrooke (?)/ Markham Hotel, 1882— demolished.

James Duff (?)/Windsor Hotel, 1880–demolished.

The Windsor Hotel, designed by James Duff of Chicago but possibly built or supervised by Edbrooke,[4] had some resemblance to the Tabor Grand Opera House in massing, but its style was more decidedly Second Empire. The mansard roof predominated and there were no gothic arches. Each floor was treated as a unit with its own type of window detailing, resulting in a facade which was diffuse and confusing when compared to the facade of the Opera House. There were at least fourteen different window shapes in the Windsor Hotel, compared to two or three at the Opera House.[5] The Tabor Grand Opera House amply displayed Edbrooke's powers as a commercial architect; his unification of the upper floors into single compositional groups and his use of regularized window sizes gave proof of his considerable advantage as a designer over Duff.

The First Baptist Church, 1883

Very little is known about Edbrooke's career between 1879 and 1883. The Tabor buildings must have kept him busy throughout 1879 and into 1880, and he may have designed the remodeled Markham Hotel, which was completed in 1882 and successfully turned an old street building into a smaller, more elegant version of the Windsor Hotel. Its detailing was reminiscent of the Tabor Block and anticipated the First Baptist Church, and Edbrooke, with his acknowledged skill in construction and his design association with the Tabor buildings, would have been the logical local choice for this job. In any case, Edbrooke's career must have been active in 1880, for in 1881 his brother arrived and the two men rented adjoining offices in the Tabor Block. Unfortunately there is no evidence of any building from this period, and the earliest dated building designed solely by Frank E. Edbrooke was the First Baptist Church, dedicated in 1883.

The church, like the Tabor Opera House of 1879-80, had an extraordinarily active surface of red brick and limestone. In spite of the cathedral facade massing and some attempt at gothic detail, the building was unecclesiastical in its effect. The frontal gable had no structural significance and was backed up by a chateau roof parallel to the false front gable. The ornamental roof refused to allow the eye either to move back along the gable or to identify the nave of the church. The whole building was obviously conceived in the same spatial terms as a commercial structure, bearing marked similarity to the Tabor Opera House in style, massing, materials, and detail. The church, which had a huge and gaudy interior, was actually a decorated shed (to borrow Robert Venturi's useful term), its false front fusing the elements of a Second Empire commercial structure and a gothic cathedral. The gothic arches were applied over rounded arches and had no structural or compositional significance; they were merely symbols for "church." Even the limestone banding had more decorative than structural significance; it involved the brick in a frenzied figure-ground relationship, cut the pilasters in half, slipped backward and forward between levels of the facade, and succeeded in completely confounding the eye.

The stylistic and compositional nervousness of Edbrooke's earlier Denver buildings dwindles considerably after the First Baptist Church, and his architecture from 1884 to the decline of his mature career in 1895 or 1896 can be separated neatly into functional types. His houses of the middle eighties participated in the later

Frank E. Edbrooke/First Baptist Church, 1883–demolished.

Queen Anne "revival," his churches began to look like churches and not like office blocks in disguise, and his commercial structures began a fourteen-year evolution from the Tabor Grand Opera House to his masterpiece, the Brown Hotel of 1890-92.

The Middle Eighties:
The Chamber of Commerce Building

Frank E. Edbrooke's first advanced and decidedly important commercial structure was, appropriately, the Chamber of Commerce headquarters in Denver. The three and one-half story building occupied a site at the corner of 14th and Lawrence Streets. Although the building was dated 1884 on its Lawrence Street facade, an 1885 photograph shows it in the middle stages of construction.

The building must have represented a decided advance in Edbrooke's career. Gone were the pseudo-gothic details and the Second Empire massing. Instead, a noble two-story arcade with rounded arches rose above a segmentally arched basement level and the building concluded in a cornice-story with paired-arch windows and an extremely simple bracketed cornice. The building was of astonishing simplicity for its date. Had it been constructed two years later, architectural historians would refer to either the Field Warehouse by Richardson or the Chicago Auditorium by Sullivan. There are, however, virtually no clear precedents for this small masterpiece of Edbrooke's middle career. Its division into three clear regions had no precedent in Richardson's career and only one or two minor precedents in Sullivan's. It seems very unlikely that the Edbrooke Chamber of Commerce Building derived, for

example, from Sullivan's 1884 Ryerson Building in Chicago, in spite of the fact that the latter structure had a tripartite vertical facade division.

The Chamber of Commerce Building must have been the queen of Denver's streets for several years after its completion in late 1885. No building in town shared its monumental simplicity of conception and execution. The smallish rusticated stones were tightly laid to avoid the loose, surfacy quality so common to Denver's later stone commercial structures. The floor-line between the first and second stories was amply recessed and gave the arches a grand structural separateness and visual strength. Each bay was identical, and there were no attempts to give the facade an episodic and picturesque variety. Segmental arches at the basement level pushed together forcefully beneath the weight of the upper stories, and the monumental arches of the arcade distributed the massive weight of the third story with poise and assurance. The Chamber of Commerce Building was probably among the most stylistically advanced structures built in the United States in the middle 1880's.

The Essex Building

Edbrooke's career between 1885 and 1889 failed to respond to the excellence of his Chamber of Commerce Building. The 1887 Essex Building was a case in point. Six stories high, it was Edbrooke's tallest building to that date and was probably the most successful commercial structure from his office between 1885 and 1889. Its facade had none of the grandeur of the Chamber of Commerce Building and possessed several "regressive" elements which were to continue almost throughout

Frank E. Edbrooke/ Chamber of Commerce Building, 1884—demolished.

39

Frank E. Edbrooke/Essex Building, 1887–demolished.

Edbrooke's career. The most obvious of these hold-overs was the frontpiece, expressed in this building by a tentative false gable over the central bay, a miscalculated compositional event which trivialized the more admirable facade.

Edbrooke's problem in the design of this facade was that of strengthening a tall, thin, and, to the nineteenth century eye, visually unstable rectangle. His choice of long, narrow arches compounded the problem rather than solving it, and the architect responded to this compositional mistake by strengthening every possible horizontal. The pilasters were treated with rusticated bands so that the eye jumped across the windows to complete the horizontal stripes visually. Cornice features predominated in the lower stories of the building, and the floor bands on the upper stories, which had been recessed in the Chamber of Commerce Building, were brought to the surface in the Essex Building. The visual effect of this horizontal-vertical tension helped

to counter the wobbly and unstable character of the facade itself.

The major advance exhibited by the Essex Building was its frank acceptance of the steel frame underneath. The attempt at building a massive and self-supporting wall *around* or *in front of* a steel-frame building was an important strengthening device in commercial architecture of the middle and later eighties. Even though Edbrooke sheathed the Essex Building in stone, he followed the narrowness of the girders so carefully and left so much of the facade open for windows that the stone facade-structure hardly appears to be holding anything up.

By 1889, Edbrooke was considered Denver's most important commercial architect. A list of buildings either in construction or in design during that year includes many of his best and largest commercial structures— the McPhee Block, the Ernest and Cranmer Block, the People's National Savings Bank, the Masonic Temple, the Metropole Hotel, and many smaller business blocks or warehouses. There was certainly too much work for one man, and Edbrooke's office was known as a starting place for many later prominent Denver and regional architects such as Fred Hale and J.J. Huddart.[6]

Edbrooke's buildings between 1889 and 1893 are difficult to divide chronologically and the commercial buildings are best discussed in smaller subgroups. Chicago provided the major aesthetic influence for Edbrooke's commercial works. His office blocks and street buildings evidence familiarity with the architecture of Louis Sullivan and, in some cases, Daniel Burnham. He shared their concern with the regularization and simplification of building forms, with the so-called integration of ornament, and with the external embodiment of the steel grid structure.

Edbrooke's aesthetic reliance on more famous Chicago architects must not, however, be exaggerated. Although certain of his buildings cannot be divorced from specific prototypes in Chicago, which was by 1890 the most booming city in America, a great deal of his work preceded or was almost exactly contemporary with architecturally famous Chicago structures. It is tempting to see Edbrooke as a provincial architect who replicated more advanced structures from the well-known architectural center of Chicago, but this reading of his career would be distinctly exaggerated. Edbrooke inhabited the same milieux, subscribed to the same magazines, and built buildings for people similar to those served by Louis Sullivan, Daniel Burnham, and the less well-known commercial architects of Minneapolis. He was not an artistic latecomer; rather, he was part of the little-understood architectural renaissance which altered American cities from the death of Richardson in 1886 until World War I.

The Frontal Light Well:
Ernest & Cranmer Building,
McPhee Block, and the Metropole Hotel

In 1889, F.E. Edbrooke and Company began three structures which were variations on the same building type, the office block with a long, narrow light well. This device provided light and ventilation for office blocks with unusually large spaces on each floor and was common in the commercial architecture of the 1870's and 1880's. Generally the light well was located at the rear of the building and was not visible from the street. Reasons for hiding the light well were undoubtedly economic; the stone or brick street-front finish of the building was less expensive if it covered only two sides on a corner building rather than bending back into a light well. Minimizing the surface area to be "finished" was a guiding principle of commercial architecture before the latter 1880's, when an increase in the surface area covered in good brick or stone began to give buildings a new luxury.

The Metropole Hotel, the McPhee Block, and the Ernest and Cranmer Block were early examples of the frontally exposed and finished light well, although there are buildings which accomplished this "turnaround" slightly earlier.[7] The McPhee Block and the Ernest and Cranmer Block were almost exactly comparable structures. Both buildings were finished in rusticated stone on the first two floors and smooth-finished sandstone on the upper stories. The middle stories of each were grouped vertically into a single section and horizontally into discrete regular bays. The top story was treated as part of the cornice, and both the buildings read in three vertical sections (base, middle floors, and top) analogous to a column's base, shaft, and capital. The frontal light well divided and lessened the massiveness of a predominantly horizontal building by splitting it visually into two sections.

The Ernest and Cranmer Block, begun in 1889, was probably the earlier of the two buildings. It was first mentioned in the March 1889 issue of the *Western Architect and Building News* and was built in the "Chicago-style" idiom common to many of Edbrooke's structures of 1889 and 1890. The office floors of the building were recessed behind large pilasters topped by rather flat Richardsonian arches, producing a predominantly vertical structure which led the eye upward along the pilasters toward the dancing arches rather than along each floor line. At the main entrance a rusticated arch was joined by a smooth stone gable, appearing to spread apart the halves of the office building and dramatize the act of entrance.[8] This entrance "event" obviously derived from Edbrooke's earlier use of the entrance tower or pavilion.

The McPhee Block was first mentioned in the *Western Architect and Building News* in October of 1889 and again in October of 1890. It differed from the Ernest and Cranmer Block in that it had a much shallower and less shadowy surface. The cornice was decidedly more restrained and the building had no softening grille or balustrade on the top. The arch at the entrance was not rusticated and was treated in a more sober, classical style. Even the tripartite windows on the top floor were separated from one another by stern and almost "correct" doric columns. The sobriety and sheer massiveness of the McPhee Block had very little precedence

Frank E. Edbrooke/McPhee Block, 17th and Glenarm Streets, circa 1889.

Frank E. Edbrooke/Ernest & Cranmer Building, 1889-90 —demolished.

in Denver architecture of the preceding decade. The Field Warehouse by Richardson and Sullivan's Auditorium were extremely solid and had very restrained cornices, but the massiveness of these buildings was countered by the lively surface rhythm of their arcades. Perhaps only the influence of McKim's more academic classicism or even William Le B. Jenney's startlingly simple Second Leiter Building of 1889-90 could explain Edbrooke's new seriousness.

We must not condemn Edbrooke too soon for becoming witless and dull. At the same time he was working on the McPhee Block, the construction of the most whimsical of all his commercial designs was being completed. The Metropole Hotel and its attraction, the Broadway Theater, formed one of the wonders of nineteenth century Denver architecture. The hotel formed a relatively thin vertical facade in the middle of the block between 17th and 18th Streets on Broadway. It lacked the three-quarter massiveness of a corner building and in spite of its relatively imposing stone facade it was an active and unstable mass. The long dark shadow of the light well was almost as wide as the two "towers" on either side and assumed a large role in the composition. Unlike the McPhee or Ernest and Cranmer Blocks, in which the mass of the two "halves" is overwhelming, the effect of the Metropole Hotel was of two long and almost wobbly rectangles on either side of a hole, or airspace. Edbrooke encouraged this rather excited reading of the building by his use of the Venetian ogee arch in addition to the more sober and traditional round arch associated with Richardsonian Romanesque. The Metropole Hotel had little of the Romanesque about it in spite of its cavernous entrance arch, and Richardson would probably have been appalled by its instability and silliness. Its windows simply floated on the smooth and spatially recessive surface of the building. There was little of the structural imagery which is evident in Edbrooke's best or more usual commercial structures. Rather, the Metropole Hotel was conceived in somewhat the same exuberant spirit as the Windsor Hotel or the Tabor Grand Opera House. Its silhouette was active against the sky, and it had an unusual variety of decorative windows for an Edbrooke building. Inside the hotel the Broadway Theater was even more extravagant and exciting. The ornament seemed to glow nervously with its own sparkly light against the predominant darkness, and the room which Sandra Dallas termed that "Meccan horror" was in keeping with the exotic ogee arches and towered facade outside.

Stylistic Discontinuities:
The People's Bank and the Masonic Temple

It is tempting to elevate Edbrooke himself to major status by declaring him to be the design partner. However, the evidence of the buildings themselves seems slightly counter to this idea of a single designer.[9] The variation in style among Edbrooke's buildings is evident in the McPhee Block, the Ernest and Cranmer Block, and the Metropole Hotel— all built within the same two-year period around 1890. There was a corresponding variation in quality or consistency in Edbrooke's work. The Masonic Temple of 1888-89, for example, is confused and lacking in unity, and is difficult to consider as the product of the same man who designed a corner block as advanced as the People's National Savings Bank of 1889-90. Both were large "street buildings," but the functional requirements of the Masonic Temple were considerably more complex.

The People's National Savings Bank was among Edbrooke's most successful buildings of any size in any material— a worthy successor to Denver's brick architecture of the 1860's. The cornice and a great deal of the ornament were designed to glorify the brick itself with no reference to the stone carver or the terra cotta manufacturer. Edbrooke had by this time begun to think of the corner building as a single object rather than as an agglomeration of distinct and separable masses. Its vertical rise, while broken into dramatic segments, was clear and consistent. The corners were

Frank E. Edbrooke/Metropole Hotel, now Cosmopolitan Hotel, 1889-90.

Frank E. Edbrooke/Facade detail, Metropole Hotel (Cosmopolitan Hotel), Broadway between 17th and 18th Streets, 1889.

*Frank E. Edbrooke/
Interior of the Broadway
Theater, 1889.*

Frank E. Edbrooke/People's National Savings Bank, 1889-90 —demolished.

strengthened by Edbrooke's use of a stylistically retard-ataire corner tower, which objectified and defined the building mass. The central tower or frontpiece was present in vestigial form on the main facade, but extended only half way up the building. Although its more finicky detail and tripartite fenestration were somewhat inappropriate to the massiveness and solidity of the building as a whole, it provided a link between the second and third sections of the building and intensified the building's verticality.

Compared to the subtle and relatively advanced People's National Savings Bank, the Masonic Temple seems flat, unduly complex, and stylistically uncoordinated. The formal division of the upper stories into corner towers flanking a central arcade may be derived from Venetian prototypes made famous by the publication of Ruskin's *Stones of Venice* in 1851. This volume was popular in America and probably influenced the massing of commercial buildings like Richardson's Cheney Block of 1875-76 in Hartford.[10] Edbrooke's use of the device in the Masonic Temple was unique in his architecture of the pre-crash period. It might, therefore, be considered as arising from the building's unusual function in downtown Denver. The Masons, of whom Edbrooke was a member, had begun to exert a tremendous force on American society by the later 1880's, and the presence of a Masonic temple in the guise of a commercial structure on a busy corner in

Frank E. Edbrooke/Masonic Temple, 1614 Welton, 1889.

Frank E. Edbrooke/Entrance to the Masonic Temple, 1614 Welton, 1889.

downtown Denver indicates the financial power of the organization. However, Edbrooke's attempt to use a tall, rectangular commercial design for a more ceremonial building was not totally successful. The use of rusticated stone throughout the facade weakened the structure owing to the visual predominance of an active and unstable shadow pattern, and the entire surface appears to wobble slightly. The rusticated "pilasters" supporting the large, smooth stone arches read more like thin walls than weight-bearing pilasters. The recession of the floor lines behind the arches is almost non-existent, and the whole side facade looked extremely thin and unsupported. The building does not "step" back comprehensively like the Ernest and Cranmer Block or the People's National Savings Bank; instead it almost seems to push outward toward the facade as if there were no structure underneath. The entire character of the building as facade is intensified by the use of false-front gables above the arches on the towers of the main facade.

In designing the Masonic Temple, Edbrooke reverted to an earlier and more complex style. He was not designing a simple office structure with identical floors containing large and undifferentiated spaces. He was designing a three-story commercial building on top of which he had to place a richly decorated and functionally complex ceremonial structure. Each floor of the upper "temple" had a rigid and varied set of smaller rooms, to which Edbrooke responded by dividing the mass into segments or sub-blocks as he had in the earlier Tabor Grand Opera House.

The long list of successful commercial structures which came from Edbrooke's office in the early 1890's stemmed directly from the People's National Savings Bank. The influence of this building on Denver architecture was both great and sudden, as evidenced by a photograph taken on California Street in the middle 1890's. The buildings are of dark red brick and stone, and their tough yet graceful facades recall the People's National Savings Bank very strongly. This type of commercial architecture, although deriving in large part from Chicago, had a toughness of detail combined with a gentleness of scale which was peculiar to Denver commercial architecture. The stony and obdurate presence of the wall which one feels so strongly in H.H. Richardson's masterpiece, the Field Warehouse, was softened and humanized in Denver. Rusticated stone, a popular material in Denver during the late 1880's and early 1890's, was rarely used in tall commercial structures except on the first or second floors.[11] The smaller

and lighter arches of brick Richardsonianism were preferred. The commercial architecture of Denver was not, however, as decorative or airy as the more famous buildings of Louis Sullivan. The visually load-bearing wall was a *sine qua non* of Denver architecture of this period. There was none of the tensile lightness of Sullivan's or Daniel Burnham's later structures in which steel technology found its way to the exterior of the building. Denver's commercial architecture of the 1890's was an architecture based on the wall-bearing structures of late Richardson and early Sullivan, but lightened because of the use of brick and decreased in scale. No brick building in Denver during the nineteenth century had the austere, megalomaniacal splendor of Burnham's Monadnock Block, Chicago's most notable brick building. The streets of Denver, following Edbrooke's lead, were more urbane and less frightening than the massive canyons being constructed during the same years in Chicago.

California Street, looking southwest from 17th Street, circa 1895.

The Club Building and The California Building

At least two of Edbrooke's notable buildings in this brick Richardsonian idiom are worthy of detailed discussion: the Club Building and the California Building.

The Club Building was a street building with a long rectangular facade not immediately divisible into discrete bays. Its fenestration was extremely regular, and its entrance was defined by a somewhat restrained Richardsonian arch. Edbrooke was not comfortable with an implacably repetitive facade, and his restrained false-front sign-board together with the residual protruding entrance bay gave the building a hint of bilateral

symmetry. His use of the short and generally centered entrance bay treated separately from the rest of the facade was one of the few conservative features in his commercial design of the late eighties. Its appearance in the Essex Building of 1887 was not jarring because of the stylistic and formal confusion in the rest of the building, but the entrance bay in the People's National Savings Bank was noticeably at odds with the rest of the structure. The entrance bay became increasingly precarious in Edbrooke's work as the century progressed. Strong on the side facade of the Ernest and Cranmer Block, it had a less important compositional role in the

People's Bank, and, by the early nineties, the motif disappeared entirely. Its presence in the Club Building was at most residual, and its weakening effect was countered by the strong, repetitive rhythm of the arches across the facade. In fact, the Club Building had a marked horizontality for an Edbrooke building and visually it related back to the Essex Building of 1887. Its recessed horizontal floor-lines, meeting insistently at the pilasters, were much more aggressive than the floor-lines in the People's Bank. Severe shadows from the double sills created strong and visually connected horizontals which interacted tensely with the vertical pilasters. The facade of the building was more active and exciting than any other facade from Edbrooke's mature period, and it gave the viewer a clear reading of the steel frame beneath it.

Edbrooke's most perfect and serene commercial structure was the California Building at the corner of 16th and California Streets. A slim six stories, its facade had a two-story base of rusticated stone surrounding generous store windows. The three-story arcade above was a simplified and elegant replication of the arcade in the People's Bank. Gone were the spatially aggressive pseudo-Corinthian capitals, and the cornice level was higher, simpler, and more classical. Terra cotta ornamentation was rare and restrained, and most of the architectural ornament was carefully laid brick in imitation of classical mouldings. The California Building, like the slightly earlier and more sober People's Bank, had classical objectness and solidity. It had no spiky corner towers and its entrance bay was identical in character to the other bays. The central location of the bay along the facade and its large, rusticated stone arch were sufficient indication of its importance.

Frank E. Edbrooke/Club Building, 1892–demolished.

Frank E. Edbrooke/California Building, 1892–demolished.

The H.C. Brown Hotel

Edbrooke's undisputed masterpiece and probably the greatest nineteenth century building in Denver is, of course, The H.C. Brown Hotel. Begun in 1890 and completed two years later, this building was and is one of the greatest nineteenth century commercial structures in America. Stylistically, it represented a refinement of the Field Warehouse-Chicago Auditorium styles. Its clearest and most accessible prototype was Sullivan's Auditorium, built in Chicago between 1887 and 1889 and the only

Frank E. Edbrooke/The H.C. Brown Hotel, 17th and Broadway, 1890-92.

Frank E. Edbrooke, Architect—
James Whitehouse, Sculptor/
Relief bust of H.C. Brown,
Brown Hotel, 17th and
Broadway, 1890-92.

important non-regional commercial structure published in the *Western Architect and Building News.* It was probably the best-known commercial structure of its period and by 1890 the most discussed and well-published American building since Richardson's Trinity Church in Boston of 1873-1877. Yet, like Trinity Church and in spite of its importance, Sullivan's Auditorium produced few worthy successor buildings. The Brown Hotel is certainly the finest of those which do exist and is probably less flawed in some ways than its precursor.

Sited on an irregular triangular lot on Broadway, the Brown Hotel was instrumental in the gradual move of the center of Denver's downtown east toward Capitol Hill. It was situated across Broadway from Edbrooke's earlier Metropole Hotel and dominated the area for decades. Its massive Broadway front (now sealed off) had little of the wit of the Metropole, but its nine-story, glass-roofed courtyard made up for its restrained and stony facade.

Since 1892 the Brown Hotel has stood its ground at the meeting of Denver's conflicting grids with enormous confidence and success. It is the only building on any of Denver's awkward triangular sites which uses its position to advantage. The three great corners of the building curve generously, and the architectural historian cannot help but see it as looking forward to Burnham's Flatiron Building in New York of 1902. Edbrooke's three curved "corners" which preserve the continuity of the building's stone "skin" are successful precisely because they avoid the whole problem of corners. They entice the eye around and around, forcing the viewer to complete the

building in his mind and making him constantly aware of its entire shape.

The building, as it was originally used, made few judgments about the importance of a particular facade. Each facade possessed its own ogee-arched entrance to the great glassed lobby and drew visitors from every part of town.

The facade of the Brown Hotel differs somewhat from the Auditorium in Chicago. Its great stone arches are wider, less crowded and more generous, allowing the eye to read across the length of the facade in long, leisurely rhythms. Instead of paired-arch floors above the main arcade there are two rows of plain rectangular windows in triplicates. These two floors and the smooth, refined cornice cap the building in a relaxed and horizontal fashion. The eye reads across the continuous stone surface rather than jumping from window group to window group as in the earlier Sullivan building. Edbrooke's residual entrance tower occurs on the southwest and northwest facades and is reminiscent of the entrance to the People's National Savings Bank. The Broadway facade has a fully expressed central "tower" clearly derived from Sullivan's Auditorium tower. Edbrooke, however, improved on his model by centering and shortening the tower. Sullivan's tower was awkward and overly massive. Its height and its large stone-to-window ratio gave it a heaviness which almost exploded the entire facade, and its off-axis placement added to its powerful instability as a form. In the Brown Hotel, Edbrooke used the tower motif without really building a tower. The three central bays are a combination of Edbrooke's traditional false-front sign-board and

Frank E. Edbrooke/Facade detail, Brown Hotel, 17th and Broadway, 1890-92.

Sullivan's more massive tower form. The resulting tower stabilizes the overly long facade by providing it with a generous but not excessively bulky focus for the composition.

Perhaps a word about the present condition of this most important of Edbrooke's structures would be in order. Tragically, the major central entrance on the Broadway facade has been closed, depriving the "main facade" of the building of any active significance. The exterior, while in generally good condition, has been altered in several small and significant ways during recent decades. All of the building's decorative sculpture except the now famous roundels and the sculpture around the doors has been removed, possibly necessitated by the fragile condition of the sandstone trim. Stone garlands which once graced the three corners and the Broadway entrance tower are also gone, and another casualty was the classical frieze between the sixth and seventh floors. These stone ornaments gave the massive stone building a celebratory appearance and indicated a connection between Edbrooke and the neo-Renaissance ornament of McKim, Mead, and White. These classical motifs based on curvilinear vegetable forms made the building look less severe and less like Sullivan's Auditorium than it does today. Even the huge carved sign above the Broadway entrance has been removed and modern tourists all too often think that the building's name was derived from the color of its stone now that H.C. Brown's name no longer stands out in sandstone relief.[12]

Frank E. Edbrooke/Brown Hotel, 17th and Broadway, 1890-92.

Frank E. Edbrooke, Architect—James Whitehouse, Sculptor/ Entrance ornament, Brown Hotel, 17th and Broadway. 1890-92.

Frank E. Edbrooke/Denver Dry Goods Company, 16th and California Streets, 1894.

The Denver Dry Goods Company, the Cooper Block, and the Majestic Building

Edbrooke's later commercial structures, such as the Denver Dry Goods Company, the Cooper Block, and the Majestic Building, are weakened late versions of his designs dating from the early nineties. The Denver Dry Goods building has almost no built-in structural definition. The pilasters which might have appeared to support the first cornice are banded with limestone as in Edbrooke's buildings of the early 1880's and lose their definition as whole, vertical forms. The long California Street facade is endless and monotonous. Round arches jam into their bays, more decorative than structurally valuable.

The Cooper Building was slightly more successful, but has been torn down. Its facade returned somewhat to Edbrooke's earlier complexities of massing and the use of the corner towers breaks the building into smaller sub-units. The corner tower was undergoing something of a renaissance in American commercial design of the early and middle nineties. One can find precedents in San Francisco's Mills Building of 1892, designed by Burnham and Root, as well as Chicago's Marquette

Frank E. Edbrooke/Cooper Building, 1895—demolished.

Building of 1893-94, designed by Holabird and Roche. Edbrooke was not far behind the nation's leading commercial architects of the nineties in some aspects, but the general quality of the Cooper Building was weaker and more confused than either the Marquette or the Mills Building. Edbrooke bled the tower into the round-arched region of the sixth floor, but his combination of towers, arched arcades and pilastered arcades was not expertly handled and the building had a flatness reminiscent of the earlier Masonic Temple.

Frank E. Edbrooke/Majestic Building
209 16th Street. The Majestic Building is one of Edbrooke's most confusing and fussy commercial structures. Its ornament, coloring, and odd shape make it one of the most exuberant buildings constructed in Denver during the nineteenth century. 1894.

Institutional Architecture:
Unity Temple, Central Presbyterian Church,
and Loretto Heights

Edbrooke was not Denver's leading designer of institutional architecture. Although he did build a number of hospitals, churches, and schools, it was his commercial architecture which engendered public admiration most. His earlier institutional architecture was generally High Victorian and less distinguished than his commercial design. The First Baptist Church, with all its stylistic and compositional confusions, has already been discussed. Two similar buildings of an institutional type, probably from the early eighties, were the first wing of the Denver County Hospital and the Insane Ward of the Arapahoe County Hospital. Neither building was particularly interesting or advanced by national standards.

Edbrooke's most important instituitonal architecture was constructed between 1887 and 1892. The three buildings which form this group are the Central Presbyterian Church, Loretto Heights College for Women, and the Unity Temple. Both the former buildings are standing; the latter, which stood at the corner of 19th and Broadway, has been demolished. The three buildings are Edbrooke's most decidedly Richardsonian structures. The first of these structures was the Unity Temple, completed in 1887. Its gabled facade was finished in brick and rusticated stone, like most of Edbrooke's buildings, but relates rather closely to Richardson's five libraries of the late seventies and early eighties. These buildings had become the predominant model for small library structures in America by the late 1880's. The Unity Temple probably derived from two of the library structures, the Ames Memorial Public Library of 1877 and the Billings Library for the

University of Vermont of 1883. The massing of the temple, its horizontal bands of stone, and is ornament are all strikingly similar to the Ames Library, which was extensively photographed in an 1886 folio from a series called *Monographs of American Architecture* published by the *American Architect and Building News.*

Edbrooke's two largest institutional structures were the Central Presbyterian Church of 1890-92 and the College for the Sisters of Loretto of 1890-91. These two buildings were comparable in size, style, and function, and were obviously closely related in Edbrooke's mind. Both of them seem to derive from Richardson's civic buildings rather than from Trinity Church, a building more clearly similar to the Central Presbyterian Church than to the Albany City Hall, for example. Edbrooke again crossed functional boundaries for his sources, exhibiting the relatively loose definition of the concept of propriety in nineteenth century American architecture. Central Presbyterian Church seems to have derived its massing from the Albany City Hall of 1880, but its tower seems to bear more resemblance to the tower of the Allegheny County Courthouse in Pittsburgh. The resemblance in both these cases, however, is more of a family association than a direct or close copy. The Church and its sister structure, the College of Loretto, which seems loosely based on the Allegheny Courthouse, can both be called Richardsonian without necessitating a direct connection to a specific source in Richardson's work. By 1890, more loose copies and replications of Richardson's buildings were reproduced in the architectural press than were illustrations of buildings by Richardson himself. While the Unity Temple was probably a clear and conscious homage to Richardson, the later buildings related to the general movement stemming from the master's work which controlled American architecture in the late 1880's.[13]

The Central Presbyterian Church was another of Edbrooke's masterpieces, in spite of its stylistic dependence on Richardsonianism, and is fortunately still standing in reasonably good condition. The church itself is enormous and fills the entire corner lot at 18th and Sherman Streets. The building is an almost perfect square and is basically a four-tower type with crossing gables of equal height and length. The material is native Colorado sandstone, laid in horizontal bands like Richardson's later work. The tower is huge. It rises straight from the building mass and has a daring openness quite uncharacteristic of any Richardson towers. Edbrooke again used the ogee arch, but only as a decorative device over rounded or "horse-shoe" arches. The church has a greater massiveness and grandeur than Richardson's courthouses, owing primarily to the greater surface area covered in stone and to the larger windows. Its confidence as a structure is emphasized by its equally confident hilltop site.

Frank E. Edbrooke/Unity Temple, 1887–demolished.

Frank E. Edbrooke/Iron lantern, Central Presbyterian Church, 1660 Sherman. This tower is an homage to Franklin Kidder's tower at the Asbury Methodist Church.

PHOTO: EDWARDS

Frank E. Edbrooke/Central Presbyterian Church, 1660 Sherman, 1899-92.

PHOTO: EDWARDS

55

Frank E. Edbrooke/Loretto Academy (Loretto Heights College), 1890-91.

The College of Loretto is weaker and less successful than the Central Presbyterian Church. Its gravity is seriously marred by sharp, finicky dormers crowded so closely together that they counteract the otherwise massive and simple facade. The tower may be more internal᾽ ᾽ ᾿fied than the tower of the church, but its connect.on with the building mass is awkward and abrupt. The tower does not rise naturally from the building mass as it did in earlier Richardson structures and in the Central Church.

The general massing of the College of Loretto was an Edbrooke paradigm, used again in the Catholic School for Boys on Logan Avenue between 17th and 18th Avenues and in the later West Denver High School, formerly on the corner of 12th Street and 5th Avenue. Both of these buildings were bland in spite of their symmetrical institutional severity, were reverting to aggregate planning and avoiding the unification which Richardson accomplished in his best buildings. The Catholic School for Boys was by far the more notable of the two. Its massive gables and almost over-scaled entrance arch gave a monumental order and grandeur to the small building. The windows were banded together in contrast to the more dispersed symmetry of the West High School facade.

Examined as a whole, Edbrooke's institutional architecture is of distinctly lower quality than his commercial designs. His dependence on Richardsonian designs seems more contrived than it did in his commercial architecture. With the single exception of the Central Presbyterian Church, the buildings must be seen as secondary buildings by the master of commercial architecture in Denver, good buildings and often attractively sited, but of relatively slight importance in the history of American architecture.

Frank E. Edbrooke/West Denver High School, 1893—demolished.

Frank E. Edbrooke/ Catholic School for Boys, circa 1890-91 —demolished.

Domestic Architecture

The evolution of Edbrooke's domestic architecture is remarkably similar to the evolution of his commercial and institutional architecture. In the early and mid 1880's he began to design houses in the predominant Queen Anne mode which revolutionized American domestic architecture after the Philadelphia Exposition of 1876. The Queen Anne mode was decidedly domestic, rarely appearing in either institutional or commercial architecture. Its predominant characteristics were half-timbering, exaggerated gables with panel designs, and picturesque pin-wheel plans. The style favored heavy roofs and protruding eaves. Its surface possessed a structural relief based on half-timbering, but extending to other surface motifs such as bay windows, recessed fenestration, and staircase towers. The Queen Anne style must be seen as the counterpart of the late Second Empire mode which dominated commercial and institutional design until the so-called Richardsonian Romanesque became fashionable in the later 1880's.

Edbrooke's earliest documented Queen Anne houses probably date from the middle of the 1880's. Five of these early houses are especially noteworthy— those of M.J. Cranmer, W.E. Parnell, G.C. Schleier, George W. Skinner and that of Edbrooke himself. All but the Skinner residence survive today. The Cranmer, Edbrooke, and Parnell residences are sited on adjacent lots in the 900 block of East 17th Avenue. These three houses are probably the latest of the group of five. Although they possess clear references to the Queen Anne style, their use of Palladian motifs and classical order suggests a slightly later date.[14]

Frank E. Edbrooke/Frank E. Edbrooke house, 931 17th Street.

The other two houses mentioned above are more pure examples of the Queen Anne style as it manifested itself in American architecture. Their spindly front porches relate to the earlier American Stick Style, as it was named by Vincent Scully, and the relative clarity of the paneled gables and half-timbering is not countered by any use of Palladian motifs. The Schleier house, which still stands on the corner of 17th Avenue and Grant Street, is by far the largest and most impressive of Edbrooke's early houses, and its position next to the larger Kountze house on the brow of the hill overlooking downtown Denver was one of the most prominent in the city during the nineteenth century. Edbrooke enlivened the Queen Anne of the house with an exotic onion tower at the corner, which served visually to anchor the shifting planes of the gables and the roof, defining the corner of the block and giving the house a gravity or groundedness lacking in the larger, towerless Kountze mansion next door. The George Skinner residence, now unfortunately demolished, was a smaller compacted version of the Schleier house with certain subtle changes which suggest a slightly later date for it. The heavy overhanging eaves of the Schleier house, so characteristic of the Queen Anne style, were replaced by a cornice, and the large paneled gables became tight and confined triangles without the paneled detail. Another significant change was the incorporation of the corner tower into the mass of the house proper. No longer a defiant and relatively distinct mass, the tower in the Skinner house was echoed by the curve of the cornice and the larger sweep of the porch. All the changes in the Skinner residence evidenced a desire on Edbrooke's part for greater unity in the design of a house and indicate a concern common in American architecture of the later part of the century for making buildings look like single objects rather than agglomerations of separate and distinct elements.

Edbrooke's houses of the later eighties and early nineties display this increasing unification of parts with greater clarity. The Frank E. Young residence, formerly at 244 West Colfax, and the Warren residence in University Park are houses of the same type and size as the Schleier residence. The Young residence, probably dating from 1888 or 1889, had many recognizable Queen Anne features. It retained the pinwheel plan and the paneled gable, but the total effect of the house was more balanced and unified. The large frontal gable was replaced by a small Queen Anne dormer; the entrance porch hugged the house mass carefully and entrance was at the center rather than the edge of the facade. The tower was constricted markedly and huddled within the silhouette of the house. The larger and somewhat flaccid Warren residence, which was completed in 1892, eschews the pinwheel plan and is a heavily roofed rectangular solid. The tower is even less apparent than it

was in the Young residence; it is a two-story bay window which balloons from the house mass rather than a separate compositional element reacting antiphonally with the rest of the house.

Frank E. Edbrooke/G.C. Schleier's residence, 1665 Grant.

Frank E. Edbrooke/George W. Skinner's residence, 1492 Race– demolished.

Frank E. Edbrooke/Frank C. Young's residence, 244 West Colfax–demolished.

Frank E. Edbrooke/Warren residence, 2160 South Cook, 1892.

Frank E. Edbrooke/East facade, Warren residence, 2160 South Cook, 1892.

Edbrooke's smaller street houses built between 1889 and 1893 are even chunkier. The B.F. Woodward House, formerly at 1530 Sherman Avenue, had no Queen Anne features. Gone were the tower at the corner, the protruding gables, the half-timbering, and the spindly wooden porch. Instead, the house was an almost implacably simple two-and-a-half story shed with the gabled end facing the street and various bays protruding timidly from its mass. The imagery of the English country house with all its bucolic rural associations was not present in this regularized urban dwelling. The house accepted its site, a small rectangular lot on a city block, with a frankness and toughness lacking in the Queen Anne houses of the earlier eighties. It possessed little architectural imagery appropriate to a home— the use of wood, the casual plan, the picturesque silhouette, the silo tower. Instead, the Woodward house was a self-consciously well-built street home with few Romantic associations. Its appearance in Denver in 1889 signaled a change in the local attitude toward the house, a change already evidenced in Richardson's houses of 1885 and 1886. This new type of house ran counter to the late Queen Anne mode in Denver throughout the late eighties and early nineties, and after the crash of 1893 Denverites accepted this new, better built, simpler, and less literary house whole-heartedly. The complexities and Romantic "excesses" of the American house of the early eighties conflicted with the desire for permanence, safety, and stability which prevailed in Denver society of the later nineties. Edbrooke, an architect whose career was dominated by the structurally rational imagery of commercial architecture, became the chief architect of post-crash Denver. His houses were emulated and further simplified by Huddart and the Baerresen brothers. The results were the street houses of upper Capitol Hill— all brick rectangles with little architectural detailing and large, heavy front porches.

Frank E. Edbrooke/W.A. Hover's residence, 1507 Lafayette— demolished.

Frank E. Edbrooke/Robert Cary's residence, 1801 Williams.

Frank E. Edbrooke/B.F. Woodward's residence, 1530 Sherman— demolished.

Frank E. Edbrooke/James E. Rhodes's residence, 1010 Pennsylvania— demolished.

The ancestors of these middle-class street homes were Edbrooke's larger gabled homes of the early 1890's. These homes, like the Charles Haskell residence formerly at 1507 Lafayette Street and the James Rhodes residence at 1010 Pennsylvania, were direct descendants of the Woodward house which was discussed above. Their gabled facades became simpler, more symmetrical and stonier as the nineties began. The Haskell house had a rusticated surface with no banding and little sculptural ornament. Its front porch was stony and over structured; the gable corners on the main facade were decorated with grimacing gargoyles, and the walls of the house were sheer, unembellished with the friendly nooks and crannies associated with the Queen Anne house.

Edbrooke's most austere residence was the James E. Rhodes house, probably built in the early nineties. The front porch had shrunk to a temple pavilion with massive ionic columns. There was no sculptural ornamentation and the stone was laid in regular, rusticated bands. The gable, a weighty and implacable triangle, was flanked by symmetrical chimneys. The image of the comfortable and casual house had completely disappeared in this forbidding, even relentless residence, which may be seen as a premonition of post-crash Denver, a city of respectable and cautious citizens.

Frank E. Edbrooke/Detail, Warren residence, 2160 South Cook, 1892.

Conclusion

Edbrooke emerges as a far more placid and less problematic architect than his greater predecessors in Chicago or his contemporaries in Minneapolis, Harvey Ellis and LeRoy Buffington. The broad outlines of his evolution from the cognate mode of the Tabor Grand Opera House to the refined Richardsonianism of the Brown Hotel are clear. The surfaces of the buildings become flatter and less concerned with active shadow relief. The "middle buildings" in this evolution are the People's Bank with its exuberant cornice and the Ernest and Cranmer Block with its broadly shadowed and lively surface. The Club Building, the Brown Hotel, the California Building, and the McPhee Block are all later and flatter; their facades have a schematic surface allusion to their massively walled precursors in Chicago of the late 1880's. This flattening or schematizing of the building surface is coupled with a gradual tendency to treat the commercial building as a single object rather than a composition of sub-units. Edbrooke fought this tendency in his design by retaining the residual "entrance tower" as a separated and often slightly protruding bay in his later designs. His reversion to complex massing in the 1888-89 Masonic Temple has been linked to functional problems inherent in the building and cannot be considered retardataire. Other characteristics of Edbrooke's architectural evolution in these years are

Frank E. Edbrooke/Facade detail, Oxford Hotel, 1612 17th Street, 1889-90.

regularization of the facade into equal bays, restriction of the number of window types, and diminishing use of either High Victorian or Second Empire detailing.

Frank E. Edbrooke survived the crash of 1893 with some success. His prominence in the city was preserved, and he was the pre-eminent architect of post-crash Denver as he had been the pre-eminent architect of pre-crash Denver. His buildings of the later nineties and the early years of the twentieth century are noticeably blander and probably poorer than his commercial structures of the late eighties and early nineties, but they are in no way bad buildings. Edbrooke participated in the broad evolution into a drier and more appropriate architecture which characterized almost all the architecture in America of the 1890's. He, like most of the architects of his generation who lived into the twentieth century, concentrated his efforts to refine, consolidate, and civilize American architecture. The architecture in America at the end of the century was good, solid, respectable, and almost self-consciously dull architecture, an architecture which ended an old century more than it began a new one.

The last building with which Edbrooke was personally associated was, appropriately, the headquarters for the Colorado State Historical Society finished in 1915. This building, built solidly of white Colorado marble on a granite base, is an almost archetypal institutional structure. Its cubic mass allows no protrusions save the massively columned and symmetrical temple front on 14th Avenue. Its plan is symmetrical, clear, and ample. The classical allusions are no longer piece-meal, nor are they tempered by elements of other styles from other architectural pasts. Rather, the classicism is apparently complete and almost archeological in its effect on the viewer. The building is architecturally pure and its imagery exudes a hardened pomp and grandeur. Its memorial, almost funereal appearance is appropriate both because it is a museum— a historical society— and because it was Edbrooke's self-consciously last building. His retirement in 1915 at the age of 75 was well-timed, and his architectural exit from Denver was as appropriate to the city's age as was his architectural entrance, the Tabor Grand Opera House.

Frank E. Edbrooke/Colorado State Museum, 14th and Sherman, 1916.

William Lang

The Domestic Architect

William Lang was undoubtedly the most popular and prolific designer of domestic architecture in nineteenth century Denver. His houses ranged from cottages to mansions and were constructed in every part of Denver and in most of the city's nineteenth century suburbs. In 1890, the *Western Architect and Building News* listed 43 houses designed by William Lang and his partner, Marshall Pugh, as well as several terraces, a store, a town hall, and an apartment hotel. One of Lang's larger stone houses, the Raymond house on the corner of 16th and Race Streets,

was prominently featured in that periodical, and frequent mention of Lang indicates his popularity within Denver's burgeoning and self-conscious architectural profession. His name appears as one of the charter members of the Colorado Chapter of the American Institute of Architects, established in 1892.

In spite of his prominence as an architect and taste-maker, William Lang remains mysterious and undocumented. No biographical information appears in magazines, newspapers, or travel books which describe nineteenth century Denver, no relatives of the architect remain in Denver, and no typically apocryphal stories about William Lang survive. In short, Lang is recorded only in the descriptions of his buildings in the *Western Architect and Building News* and in depersonalized listings of the *Denver Directory*.

Lang began his recorded career with a confident large-letter advertisement in the 1886 *Denver Directory* and kept his offices on the northwest corner of 17th and Curtis Streets. Nothing is recorded from these first years of practice save a drawing submitted for the Unity Temple, but an inauspicious beginning for the architect can be inferred. Denver was not enjoying a building boom in 1886 in spite of the large number of real estate transfers, and by 1885 the number of architects had dropped by half from a high of 26 in 1883. The slump continued until later in 1887, when a construction boom accompanied wild real estate speculation. Lang's small-letter listing in the 1887 *Denver Directory* corroborates this inference of an unsuccessful beginning.

The prospects for architects rose in 1888, and William Lang's move from the street building at the corner of 17th and Curtis to the old Ghost Block indicates some participation in the success of his profession. By 1889, he was truly established. Listings for that year include 35 buildings in the suburb of Berkeley (later incorporated into the Highlands) a six-story business block for his landlord, A.M. Ghost, several residences, a courthouse, St. Mark's Church, and a house for himself. Although this work of one year was far less than the yearly production of men like Edbrooke and Roeschlaub, it is impressive for an architect so young, so locally inexperienced, and so eccentric.

Lang was, undoubtedly, the most self-consciously eclectic architect in the city of Denver. He never built a building in a clear, nameable style and was an architect who conceived of a building as a combination of architectural elements derived from a great many other buildings. He exemplifies one of the two types of provincial architects active in the west during the 1880's— the eclectic and the Richardsonian. Both types of architects responded to the almost intolerable complexity of the architectural profession in fundamentally different ways. The eclectic worshipped complexity and the Richardsonian strove for simplicity.

Architects like William Lang and his lesser known partner Marshall Pugh depended on constant inspiration from beyond the confines of Denver. They were enthusiastically learning from buildings which were published in national sources and from details of these buildings. Their own architecture is inconceivable in vacuo. They saw themselves as quintessential architects who could learn from all the architecture which had ever been constructed, architects who were absolutely modern because their architecture was only possible given the most modern system of national and international communications yet conceived by mankind. Their brand of architecture— and the reader will shortly be exposed to its fabulous eclecticism— was an architecture of the melting pot. It was an egalitarian and unbiased architecture free from the imperalist imagery of the Second Empire. Its aesthetic was one of complexity, confusion, and, as Robert Venturi would no doubt add, contradiction. Its enemy was classicism, rationality, and clarity. Darkness was preferrable to light. Pattern was desired. Stained glass was used with great abandon, and the windows portrayed proto-Art Nouveau leaf forms, flower forms, geological forms, and birds. The great

William Lang/W.S. Raymond house, 1572 Race, 1890.

William Lang/Front window, Raymond house, 1572 Race, 1890.

peacock window in the staircase hall of Lang's house on the corner of 12th and Pennsylvania is almost erotic in its curves and in the sensuous sweetness of its colors. The walls glow with the internal warmth of stained wood and with the patina of varnish. Mirrors enlarged and intensified the glowing light so loved by the late nineteenth century eclectics. They made space indeterminate and almost frightening. One could peer up the stairs from the front parlor while keeping an eye on the dining room and, around the corner, on the front door— all this with many well-placed mirrors. The visitor was at the disadvantage— someone could always be watching.

This sense of the indeterminate, which was so important to architects of the later eighties in the west, motivated their choice of styles as well as their choice of materials on the interior. Lang was very rarely obtrusive with his borrowed affectations. None of his buildings give themselves away to the casual viewer like many Richardsonian buildings. One can rarely figure out what William Lang's precise sources were. He took small details and enlarged them, as well as the converse. He would so detach a motif from its context that its context could never be found again. He would violate or

William Lang/Porch column, Raymond house, 1572 Race, 1890.

William Lang/Corner chimney and gable, Raymond house, 1572 Race, 1890.

William Lang/Interior of staircase window, Raymond house, 1572 Race, 1890.

William Lang/Entrance on the north facade, Raymond house, 1572 Race, 1890.

destroy a motif for his own use and recombine it with another motif— or several motifs. In short, his architecture was absolutely unique and absolutely evasive. It was so eclectic in its combinative powers that the modern viewer is generally left with what must be an object with so many borrowings from so many different types of sources and of so many different kinds that the sources can never be fully acknowledged. William Lang was probably a master eclectic. He was certainly the finest and most complex eclectic architect who worked in Denver and, though his work is not at all well-known, he may have been one of the best late eclectic architects in the United States.

St. Mark's Church

St. Mark's Church was one of the most eclectic, most disjunctive, and least "modern" churches constructed in Denver during the nineteenth century. It was brazen and exciting, revelling in the stylistic freedoms and discontinuities allowed the architect of the late nineteenth century. St. Mark's Church exhibits the same lumpiness in its massing and the same epidermal toughness in its rusticated covering as E.B. Lamb's churches of the 1850's and 1860's in England, and is one of three or four buildings in Denver which could be called High Victorian gothic and which would be considered provincial variants of the later nineteenth century churches of

William Lang/St. Mark's Church, 12th and Lincoln, 1890.

England.[1] The incongruities of its parts and the extravagant use of protrusions, pinnacles, and window variants all point to British sources, yet the building as a whole seems remarkably American, even western American in its formal complexity and in the lack of attention to long-lasting materials. St Mark's, like many buildings in Denver, was constructed of a soft gray limestone which is susceptible to buckling and wear from the elements. Much of the architectural detailing has been lost in spite of the recent efforts to plaster the building, and the corner tower fell in the 1950's.

Lang's buildings have an almost organic quality: they appear to be shrinking and growing simultaneously. St. Mark's, while not a classic example of Lang's distortions, has many fascinating problems in scale. The smallness of the chapel, which is treated as parallel and analogous to the church itself, is made more apparent by the bigness of its buttresses. The size of the church is emphasized by elaborate small-scale aisles and side-porches which separate it from the street. Tiny gothic windows which surround the church proper contrast with the much larger, more confident windows of the nave and the northern apse. Large and small react to each other like color opposites in a painting; the small enhances the large, and the large further diminishes the small.

The interior of St. Mark's is remarkably beautiful and intimate, yet even this pleasant and attractive room is full of discontinuities and surprises. Its spiky wooden beams seem at odds with the resolute stony exterior, and weighty, clustered Romanesque columns hold up airy gothic arches. The arches point upward and the columns push down— another typical Lang tension. The rectilinear pattern of the exposed beams is visually excited by the addition of gothic roundels which appear to swirl in free circular rhythm. The nave is completed with a limpid gothic arch inset with seven thin vertical windows which serve as a natural candelabrum, compacting and intensifying the light from outside into long, thin tapers with flaming gothic tips.

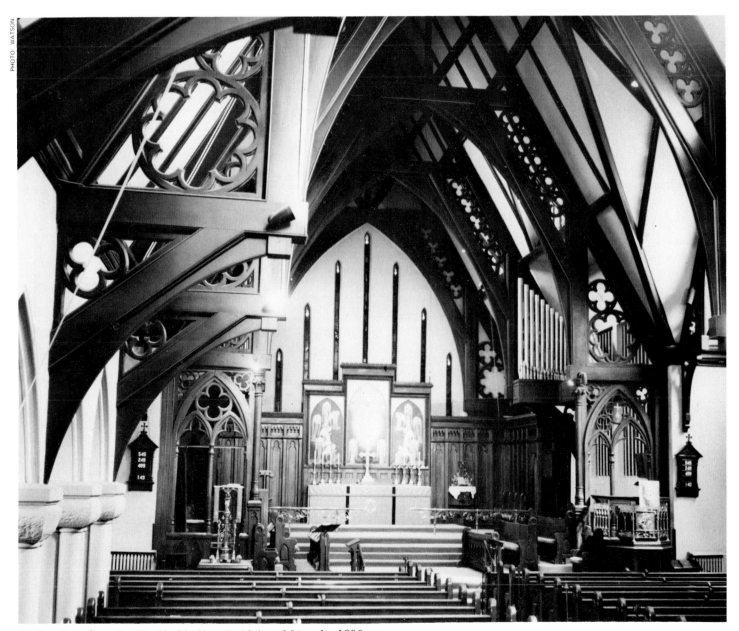

PHOTO WATSON

William Lang/Interior, St. Mark's Church, 12th and Lincoln, 1890.

William Lang/Everts house, 1889-90–demolished.

The Everts House
and the First Kittredge Residence

The Everts house and the Kittredge residence were Lang's most distinctive houses. They could only have been designed by William Lang, a remark which is not applicable to many other Denver buildings. The Everts house, which has been demolished, can be most easily understood when it is compared to the house next door, the more predictably Queen Anne Molly Brown House.[2] The roof and the facade were a complex combination of curves and straight lines, billowing forth at the front in a way very reminiscent of Richardson's 1880 Ames Gate Lodge, a building which Lang undoubtedly knew. Yet Lang's aesthetic was markedly different than Richardson's. Instead of "building up" his house in what appears to be a rational and structural manner, Lang crammed details together, used architectural elements with great expressive abandon, and in so doing altered our conception of the Queen Anne street house. The great arched window on the second floor of the west facade was overscaled and ambiguously styled. Its shape

was Richardsonian Romanesque, but spindly Queen Anne wooden supports were used beneath an aggressively mannered keystone. Even the keystone had at least a double structural function: it capped the arch and supported the miniature attic window above. Like the arches on the side aisles of St. Mark's, it weighed down and pushed up simultaneously. The same observation can be made about the thin wooden "columns" on the north facade, which seemed both to hold up the gable and to be hung from it. Their structural purpose was ambiguous and they excited the viewer's reading of the side facade.

Lang used the curved line both for its strength as a brace and for its softness, recessiveness, and elegance. The curves in the roof seemed to express an inner life, an expandability. The curves of the Palladian window expressed a geometric clarity and perfection; the curves of the outer wall pulled the visitor up the stairs and acted as a visual brace which held together or "completed" the wall. The curved stone wall on the north side of the main facade was juxtaposed against a right-angled corner of the balcony, and the right-angled corners of the chimney on the north facade were juxtaposed against the curve of the balcony.

The house built for Kittredge before the construction of his well-known "castle" in Montclair was probably the wildest small house in Denver. It competed with the McMurtrie house and Colonel Boethel's fabulous pile for the honors in tastelessness and like its larger and less interesting competitors it has been torn down. Lang's tendency to cram disparate styles and architectural elements into a single complex object reached a frenzied level in the Kittredge house. Stylistically, it was probably his most heterogeneous building. Richardsonian, Shingle Style, Queen Anne, Palladian, and castellated elements all competed. Its exotic domed tower was grafted to the mass of the house and violated the wholeness and integrity of both the Queen Anne gable and the front porch. Lang exerted supreme power over past architecture by selecting and combining elements in the most graceless possible manner. No element was allowed to stand in solitary splendor. The tower was shrunken and misshapen in comparison to the Queen Anne tower in Edbrooke's Schleier house. It struggled unsuccessfully to assert itself, seeming jammed into the body of the house. There was no use of the generous pinwheel plan with wings which spread laterally from the central staircase hall. Instead, the Kittredge house was an almost perfect rectangle from which balconies, chimneys, porch and tower all pushed with an aborted strength.

William Lang/First Kittredge residence, 1889–demolished.

William Lang/Townhouse at 1532 Emerson, 1889.

Townhouses (Rowhouses)

Lang's houses fall into two types, the free-standing street house and the rowhouse. Of the rowhouses only four remain, three on the 1600 block of Washington Street and the fourth at 1532 Emerson Street, which is the most interesting of the four.[3] Its gabled facade elaborately plays symmetry against asymmetry. The ground floor is bilaterally divided by a centered buttress which supports the second floor bay window, and a deeply shadowed entrance porch pulls the viewer's attention to the right of the centered buttress. This pull is exaggerated on the second floor by a gnome-like corner tower above the entrance porch, but the viewer's attention is pulled to the left again by the gable and its mysteriously underscaled and recessed stone porch. The center of the house is defined by a beautifully detailed bay window on the second floor which reacts intensely with the center of the gable which has its own "symmetrical features"— porch, arched window, gargoyles, and an eagle perched on top. The viewer's eye darts about the facade, into the recesses and out along the tower and the bay window, in an attempt to balance, to compose and to unify the disparate elements.

William Lang/Porch detail, townhouse at 1532 Emerson, 1889.

William Lang/Bay window, townhouse, 1532 Emerson, 1889.

William Lang/Bay window detail, townhouse, 1532 Emerson, 1889.

William Lang/Gable detail, townhouse at 1532 Emerson, 1889.

William Lang/Columns, townhouse at 1532 Emerson, 1889.

William Lang/Corner tower and gable detail, townhouse at 1532 Emerson, 1889.

The three surviving rowhouses on Washington Street were originally part of a group of five houses built in 1889 or 1890. These houses, all built by Lang, were designed in such a short time that they must be considered to be a group, responding to one another in calculated and subtle rhythms as one walked along the street. Lang began at one end with rusticated asymmetry and ended at the other with perfectly symmetry and superb balance. The houses in between read like variations on a single theme, and the razing in 1966 of two homes in the center destroyed the subtlety and power of the whole group. A description of the transformation of curves, towers, bays, styles, and compositions would be exceedingly complex. Lang progressively emphasized the gable as the viewer walked from north to south. The first house has none; the second house had a tentative, off-axis Dutch gable, the third had an almost perfectly symmetrical gable placed off-axis; the fourth has an axial and symmetrical gable with a stepped silhouette, and the fifth has a perfectly symmetrical and axial gable of the more common unstepped variety. The houses move from asymmetry to symmetry, from complexity to simplicity, from rusticated stone through smooth stone to a perfectly balanced mixture of the two.

William Lang/Rowhouses, 1600 Block Washington, 1890.

William Lang/Townhouse, 1648 Washington, 1889-90.

William Lang/Two townhouses (the one on the left was the architect's house), 1624, 1626 Washington, 1890.

William Lang/Corner detail, townhouse, 1648 Washington, 1889.

William Lang/Detail of the porch, townhouse, 1648 Washington, 1889.

William Lang/Detail of a window pair on the west facade of a townhouse, 1648 Washington, 1889.

The Bailey House

In spite of the quality and success of his rowhouses, Lang's talents were best employed in his free-standing dwellings. Of the many houses which he designed between 1889 and 1892, a large and representative group remains. The discussion of Lang's houses will focus to a large extent on these remaining structures, many of which are in an excellent state of preservation. The G.W. Bailey house at the corner of 16th and Ogden is the largest surviving house by Lang. It is sited on an earthen platform about six feet above the sidewalk in the usual manner for houses of the middle and upper-middle classes in later nineteenth century Denver. While massing is Queen Anne and includes the corner tower and pinwheel plan, Richardsonianism predominates in the materials and details. The house was described at some length in the October 1889 issue of the *Western Architect and Building News.*

"Stone residence for G.W. Bailey, on Ogden Street, to cost $30,000. Built of buff Longmont sandstone, with trimmings of blue Longmont. The parlors, library, and hall are finished in butternut; the dining room in antique oak; the chambers and upper halls are finished in satin-wood, birds-eye maple, and black ash; bathroom fitted with procelain tub and open fixtures. All work throughout the house of the best description." [4]

William Lang/Bailey house, 1600 Ogden, 1889.

William Lang/Chimney detail, south facade, Bailey house, 1600 Ogden, 1889.

This description displays Lang's love of rich materials; woods of varying colors, grains, ages, and patinas; stone of different colors and cuts; and, of course, the then modern metal plumbing exposed for everyone to see. Lang did not describe the size, the style, or the character of the house. He was not concerned in his prose with features of *design.* He was describing a fine and carefully constructed house rather than a stylistically up-to-the-minute house. He was selling his product, an almost aggressively well-built house, made of the finest materials used in the most obvious fashion. This concept of the house as a building of sound construction is crucial to an understanding of so-called High Victorian architecture in the western United States. What seem to us today to be silly, pretentious, and confused dwellings were thought of by their architects and their owners as ideal homes, built to last for generations.

The Bailey house appears to be the tamest of the residences Lang built. Ostensibly, it could have been designed by any of a number of Denver architects, including Edbrooke and Huddart. Its interest today lies in its slight exaggerations and recombinations of certain features. The cantilevered gable of the north facade hovers protectively over the bay window, combining three separate elements— gable, chimney, and bay window— into a single composition. The notion of a multi-functioning architectural element is implicit here. The chimney is more than a chimney; it is a structural vertical which holds up a dangerously protruding gable, and as a compositional unit it acts as the center of a bilaterally symmetrical grouping of windows. Examined in detail, the Bailey house is almost as rich in Lang's combinations of imagery and styles as his smaller houses. Its large size and grandeur probably forced the architect to accept the more generous Queen Anne massing which makes the house appear more conservative than it is in fact.

The Vine Street Group

A group of three Lang houses survives on the 1400 block of Vine Street. These three houses and a corner house, now demolished, formed a single group and, like the group on 17th Street by Edbrooke and like Lang's own Washington Street rowhouses, appear to have been designed in an architectural conversation. However, they were probably not all designed at the same time. The J.A. Tedford house at 1415 Vine was mentioned in the July 1889 issue of the *Western Architect and Building News* and cost $10,000 to build. The O.P. Grove residence at 1435 Vine was built late in 1890 and cost an inflated $18,000. The house between them, 1429 Vine, is not mentioned in the literature, but is clearly part of the group and must be assigned to William Lang as a probable speculation building.[5]

William Lang/Tedford residence, 1415 Vine, 1889.

The Tedford house is the most traditional of the three in its use of Queen Anne and Richardsonian imagery. It was constructed with a pseudo-rusticated brick which may have been made to order for Lang; it was not used extensively by other architects. While greatly decreasing the cost of the house, this brick gave the surface the same nervous and wobbly shadow as the more expensive rusticated stone which Lang favored in the later eighties. The house is typically quirky, although it lacks the brilliance and the exuberance of the Everts and Kittredge residences. The daring and unprecedented placement of the tower over the hollow of the porch is the oddest feature of the house and is not as successful as it might be.

The house next door seems to be an improvement, even a comment on the Tedford residence. Its corner tower is laterally placed so as to engage the stumpy and unsupported tower of the Tedford residence in conversation. Its dominating gable uses the features of the Queen Anne gable which the Tedford residence lacks, and is compositionally stronger and cleaner. The chimney appears mysteriously from a blank brick wall at the attic level and is held in check by the strong horizontal and vertical pattern of the half-timbering. The porch is more generous and deeply shadowed than the porch of the Tedford residence, and the large oak door, recessed from the facade, gives the relatively planar house an aura of great depth and size.

William Lang/Tedford residence, 1415 Vine, 1889.

William Lang/Corner tower and balcony, house at 1429 Vine, 1890.

The Grove house is the most unusual and probably the latest of the group. Its entire composition seems to respond to the dominant Queen Anne gable. It sits grandly in the middle of the block, favoring neither side and forming a climax to the group. The shadows of the gable play across the curved shingle wall beneath, giving the surface a liveliness typical of Lang houses. The Grove house, like the Emerson Street rowhouse, shows a compositional concern with symmetry and asymmetry. The protruding bay on the second floor is balanced by a recessed balcony, and the attic dormers symmetrically exaggerate the angle of the gable. The whole house seems to explode from within, pushing out at every possible place and spreading to overflow its confined city lot. In a way, the Grove house is an enormous rowhouse, and it must be seen in strong contrast to the Queen Anne asymmetry of the free-standing Tedford residence. William Lang mixed his modes with extraordinary wit in both the Washington Street rowhouse group and the Vine Street free-standing house group. He designed rowhouses to look like free-standing houses and free-standing houses to look like rowhouses. Both

William Lang/Grove residence, 1435 Vine, 1890.

PHOTO: EDWARDS AND BROWN

William Lang/Porch detail, Grove residence, 1435 Vine, 1890.

groups show the same concern for a lateral architectural progression from asymmetry to symmetry, from tower to gable.

Plans and Interiors

Although a large, even a representative sample of Lang's houses remain, none of these houses are single family dwellings today. With the exception of the Bailey house, which contains offices, all Lang's masterpieces are now rooming houses and cannot be viewed today in their original glory. Their staircase halls, which are for the most part intact, have been closed in on the second floors due to fire laws for multiple-unit dwellings. The doorways between rooms have been built up. Bathrooms have been added and walls destroyed with coats of plaster. Though the situation is far from hopeless, it is difficult for the architectural historian to arrive at a complete understanding of the interior of Lang's houses. Photographs are not extant, and only the Kittredge house, which is now destroyed, has published floorplans. If the staircase halls which do survive are any indication, and they must be a very good indication, Lang's houses had among the most lavish, dark, and beautifully detailed interiors built in the city of Denver in the 1880's and early nineties. Each house is different.

1435 Vine

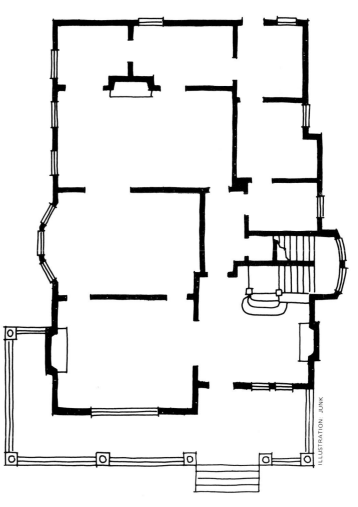

Each has its own peculiar flavor. Each staircase hall is designed to compliment the house for which it was designed. Lang's interiors seem to have been as unique and diverse as his exteriors. It is a pity that the modern historian cannot discuss them more fully.

In spite of the changes made on the interior of William Lang's houses, it is still possible to derive approximations of the original plans of these houses. The method involved is very little different from archeology: mouldings are traced; the patterning of floor boards is followed; closets are opened; and the remains of rooms are analyzed for internal consistency. Oftentimes, the results are bafflingly vague. The magnificent staircase in the house at 1460 High Street was totally dis-assembled and re-assembled sometime in the early twentieth century. A complete reconstruction of the design for this staircase would take days, possibly months of detailed examination, measuring, and analysis. These thorny problems aside, a general and occasionally a very good idea of these plans can be ascertained, and the results are worthy of discussion.

William Lang was not particularly innovative in his house planning. The nineteenth century, most particularly the 1880's, was a period of rapid and influential development in the history of the house plan. As the century progressed, the finicky arrangement of rooms characteristic of planning in the mid-century gave way to more generous, larger, and more clearly organized spaces. Large houses for very wealthy clients often had only three or four major spaces on the main floor. The entrance hall was emphasized, and the staircase became more dramatic. Landings were enlarged; doors and windows were widened; and stairs were made broader and lower. All of these innovations appear in William Lang's houses of the later eighties, but somewhat after the period of their invention and proliferation on the east coast. His houses, regardless of their budget or square footage, contained a hall, a front reception room, a parlor, and a dining room on the main floor. In addition, a kitchen space, which varied in size and complexity from house to house, was situated at the rear of the house with its own separate entrance and staircase.

This program was certainly not advanced or unusual in American architecture of the later eighties. Lang's plans, very like his exteriors, were notable for their subtle details rather than for their originality of conception. He was an architect who designed buildings which were complex, but conventional objects. His architecture was an inclusive art, an art based on all past

1460 High

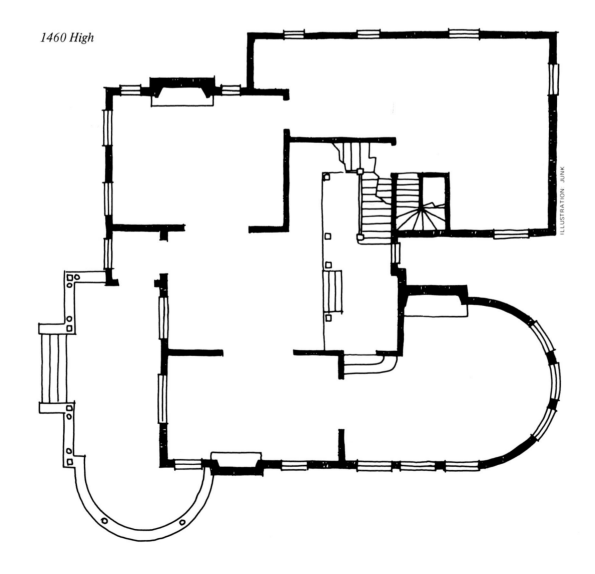

ILLUSTRATION JUNK

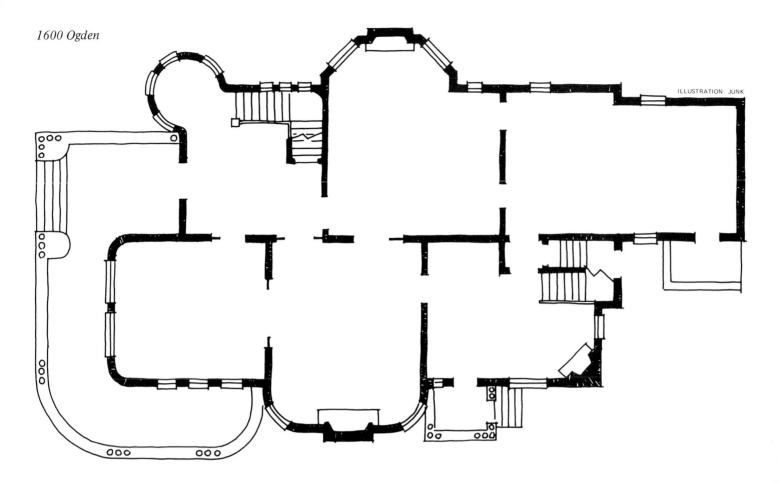

ILLUSTRATION: JUNK

architecture, rather than a reductive art designed to redefine human action. Lang's houses, unlike Richardson's, White's, or Wright's, did not re-evaluate the idea of the house. Instead, Lang designed houses which departed from convention in very subtle ways. He must be seen, in his facades as well as his plans, as a late perfector of the High Victorian eclectic house rather than an innovator.

1429 Vine

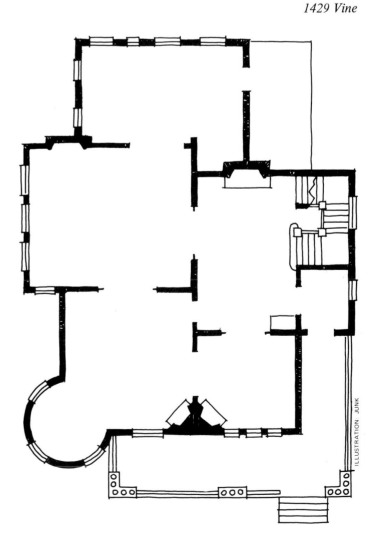

Because of the narrow frontage which had become conventional in Denver lot planning by the mid 1870's, Lang's houses stretch back on the lot. There are generally only two rooms facing the street— the hall and the reception room— with a buffering front porch. The houses were often divided roughly in half by a long continuous wall frequently interrupted by doors. This device is seen most clearly in the plan of the Bailey house at 16th and Ogden Streets, but is also present in the houses at 14th and Josephine, at 1429 Vine, and, to a lesser extent, in the Grove residence at 1435 Vine. This spine was countered by an active differentiation of the size, shape, and detailing of the major rooms. The visitor generally entered on axis and was directed laterally to the reception room. His movement into the house was generally through rather than along the center spine, and the spine, while apparent in plan, is not apparent as the visitor moves throughout the house. The general effect of Lang's houses is of tightly organized and controlled complexity. He managed to congeal four or five varied rooms into a nearly rectangular plan. The shape of the lot exerted an urbanistic

ILLUSTRATION: JUNK

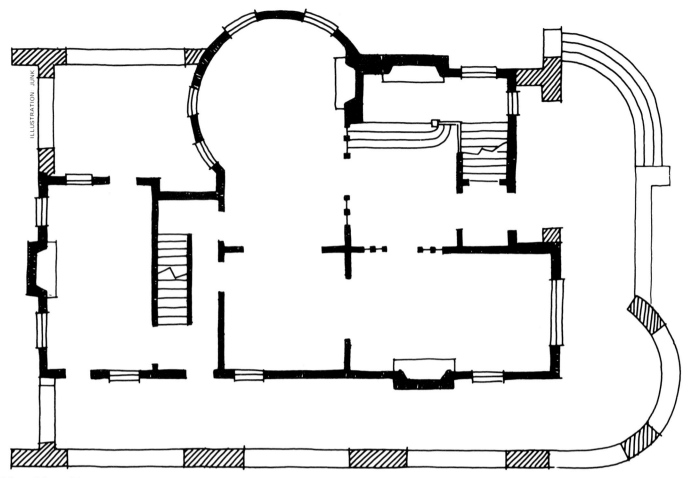

14th and Josephine

pressure on the shape of the plan, and the shape of each room exerted pressure on the basically rectangular envelope of the building. The inside burgeoned out—dormers, bay windows, towers, and projecting porches—and was countered by the resolute boxiness of the urban requirement in Denver. As a result of the high cost of real estate and the bleak character of the plains, Denver's lots had been small and narrow since the founding of the city in 1858. Very few houses built in the city during the nineteenth century, regardless of their cost, could really be called mansions or estates. They were city dwellings with narrow street fronts and carriage houses at the rear. The character of their plans was influenced by these urbanistic constrictions, and the task of the architect was to design a varied, exciting dwelling on a 50 by 100 foot lot.

On the interior, Lang's houses often appear to be larger than they are because of the variety in shape and character among the rooms. The use of mirrors, large sliding doors, transoms, extended bay windows, and varnished woods gave the rooms in Lang's houses the edgeless and indeterminate character already mentioned earlier in the chapter. Space flowed mysteriously through the rooms, and the houses were extremely unified. Doors were wide and gave the rooms very little separateness. One could view at least two and often three other rooms from any one room on the main floor. Yet, there was an enormous flexibility; the heavy

sliding doors permitted the owner to close himself off when he wished. Any room could be separated from or integrated with any of the adjacent rooms. Form did not follow function in the same way as it does in the twentieth century.

The conversation between curves and straight lines which animated the exterior of so many Lang houses plays an equally important role in the plans of those houses. Lang's more expensive houses of the early nineties like the Raymond house, the Bailey house, and the un-named house at the corner of 14th and Josephine have a remarkable complexity of plan. The bay window on the north facade of the house at 14th and Josephine swoops around and into the house mass and is countered by the conventional rectangular character of the room. The outer walls of the reception room and the parlor of the Bailey house curve gracefully in opposition to the rectangular corners at the other ends of the rooms. The porch and the parlor of the house at 1460 High push out from the mass of the building and recall the pin-wheel plan which was common earlier in the eighties. The freedom of the curve is juxtaposed by Lang against the control of the rectangle. He was not, however, a proponent of the undisciplined or totally free curve. Like most architects whose work stems from the drafting process, he created his curves from perfect circles. They have a geometric clarity which combines with their delicacy and wit to form a highly complicated

William Lang (?)/Residence at 12th and Pennsylvania, circa 1890.

image. They defy the rectilinear objectness of the house by pushing out and pulling in, by freeing themselves from the constraints of the conventional plan.

On viewing Lang's plans as a whole, the casual viewer is at once struck by their variety and graphic attractiveness. Lang obviously spent a great deal of time on his house plans and produced houses which suited the character, the budget, and the tastes of his client. He was not a hack domestic architect like so many local designers who produced hundreds of nearly identical dwellings in the same year. He was not obsessed with a single house type in spite of the uniformity in program which is clearly observable in his houses. If one were to read a list of the rooms in each of Lang's houses with a description of their character, but without a discussion of their relative location, all the houses would sound the same. Lang's plans individualized and enlivened his programs to a greater degree than the plans of any other architect in the city during his career.

A complete coverage of the surviving Lang houses exceeds the limits of this short study. The Raymond house at the corner of 16th and Race Streets is notable for its beauty and interest as an architectural artifact, and its position on the same side of the same block as the Henry Bohm residence at 1524 Race suggests that these two houses and their unattributed neighbors formed another William Lang group. Such groupings were common in the nineteenth century and architects often are listed as having built or designed two, three or more adjacent houses for the same speculator. The large gray house on the corner of 12th and Pennsylvania Streets and the house at 1457 Race were probably also built by Lang, although they are not mentioned in the *Western Architect and Building News*, the only reliable source available to the modern historian.

Oddly, Lang and his partner Marshall Pugh did not build extensively for Denver's wealthiest residents, who often preferred to use eastern architects. Lang and Pugh

were the architects for the new upper-middle class which emerged during the 1880's, and the only mansion to their credit was built on Corona Street in 1890 for William Church. One of the most successful of the Denver mansions, it was well-known to Denverites and published extensively. Its castellated exterior was grand and rugged, and the overscaled ogee arch at the entrance gave the whole building a wit absent in all of Edbrooke's larger houses. Its destruction was lamentable to say the least.

In the 1880's in Denver, the middle classes (often through local real estate speculators) became the great patrons of local domestic architecture. Lang's houses, built around their image of the ideal house, were smallish mansions, filling their city lots and pushing confidently outward from their basic rectangular foundations. They were well-built houses which proclaimed their continental and eastern sources with a freedom, even an abandon, which was lacking in the wildest architecture of the east.

William Lang (?)/Detail on the west facade of the house at 1544 Race, circa 1888.

William Lang (?)/Detail on the south facade of the house at 1544 Race, circa 1888.

William Lang(?)/Residence, 1457 Race, circa 1889.

William Lang(?)/Residence, 1457 Race, circa 1889.

The Ghost Block

Probably the most interesting of the commercial blocks from the nineteenth century which survives today is the badly damaged Ghost Building at the corner of 14th and Glenarm. Though this building is not ascribed to William Lang in any document, it is probably his only surviving commercial structure. Lang was hired to design a six story office block for A.M. Ghost on the corner of 16th and Glenarm in 1889. This building was never built, although Lang did design the Ghost house in 1890. It is probable that the size and expense of the first design was too great for Mr. Ghost, and a less expensive building was designed for another location. The resulting building derives from Edbrooke's Chamber of Commerce Building of 1884. It has the same massive arches, the same rusticated stone, and the same cornice story. Beyond these schematic resemblances, the two buildings had very little in common, Lang's surface is considerably more active and interesting. The size and visual strength of the stones counters their tendency to wobble and shift as the light changes. The building has a repetitive grandeur which is undeniable, and it is unified beneath an enormous classical cornice. The proportions lack the delicacy of Edbrooke's, and the building is definitely the strongest commercial structure of its size constructed in the city during the nineteenth century.

William Lang (?)/The Ghost Block, 15th and Glenarm. Probably Lang's only business block which survives. Circa 1891.

Conclusion

The career of William Lang came to an abrupt halt in 1893, the year of the great silver crash which so decisively affected the city of Denver. Marshall Pugh, his partner between 1889 and 1892, left the city inexplicably, and the *Denver Directory* of 1893 lists William Lang (in small print) as an architect, but his residence had changed from the rowhouse on Washington Street to a rooming house. The directory of 1894 lists no William Lang, but a W. Lang (waiter) is mentioned for the first time— and the last— in that year.

William Lang was a casualty of a dramatic change in taste caused by the severe economic depression. Denver's economy, which was based so heavily on silver mining and the silver standard, collapsed more seriously than the economies of most other major cities in 1893. The blow to the optimistic and expansive tone of the city of Denver was decisive, and an era of extreme financial and cultural conservatism began when Denver finally recovered from the crash. Indeed, the psychological damage to the city was greater and more significant than the financial damage. The crash of 1893 affected Denver's architecture more seriously than any other event in the history of the city before or since that time. Lang's architecture did not fit the newly sobered Denver as well as the severe boxes of Edbrooke, the Baerresens, and Huddart. Although Lang adopted the neo-Renaissance detail which began to replace Richardsonian and Queen Anne detail by the early nineties, he did not change his style to fit his detail.

A house of the early nineties which can surely be attributed to William Lang is evidence of the architect's continued and, by that time, inappropriate eclecticism. Still standing at 1460 High Street, this huge brick house is William Lang at his most characteristic. Styles are mixed with great abandon— Shingle Style dormers, Palladian windows, neo-classical doric columns on the porch, and a huge gothic arch on the south facade. A greatly over-scaled roof balloons from the house and reaches optimistically outward and upward. The house is anything but responsible, anything but safe, and anything but contained. It, like William Lang's other buildings, came to be associated with the irresponsibility and careless opportunism which Denverites often wrongly considered to be their downfall.

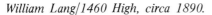
William Lang/1460 High, circa 1890.

PHOTO WATSON

Robert S. Roeschlaub

The Institutional Architect

Robert Roeschlaub came to Denver in February 1873 and found himself not only the city's first architect but its only architect. Denver was a very good place for a young architect early in 1873. The great panic of that year which so crippled the economies of the eastern and midwestern states had little effect on the stable, silver-oriented economy of Denver, and although the building boom slowed somewhat in early 1873, the great influx of "ruined" people who began to arrive late in the year created a need for new housing, retail shops, and institutions. Roeschlaub's arrival in the middle of these events proved most fortuitous, and he established a career which continued until his retirement in 1915 at the age of 72. Unlike other Denver architects in the nineteenth century, Roeschlaub lived through

every major phase of the city's economy and continued designing good buildings throughout the stylistic battle of the latter nineteenth century.

Robert Roeschalub was born in Munich, Germany on July 6, 1843.[1] His parents resettled in Quincy, Illinois in 1846, and Roeschlaub lived there until his move to Denver in 1873. He was not a roving architect like Edbrooke, who learned the trade by skipping about the country from one building boom to another, and he did not align himself with railroad culture or mining culture or pioneer culture. His architecture exhibits few traces of real influence from Chicago and he seems to have been a decidedly local architect throughout his life. His later architecture shows some Richardsonian influence, but his buildings were remarkably consistent; he was not easily influenced by trends or inclined to indulge in the various styles of the seventies and the eighties. Although he did design a few highly unusual buildings, most notably the Peter Gottesleben house, which stood at the corner of Colfax and Gilpin, most of his buildings have a respectable solidity— the mark of an architect who built to last for generations.[2]

Roeschlaub is best classed as Denver's primary institutional architect. His architectural legacy has survived well primarily because he designed so many buildings for the Denver Public Schools, including the old East Denver High Shool, Ebert, Emerson, Gilpin, Hyde Park, Longfellow, Mitchell, Moore, Whittier, Wyman, and Valverde schools. He designed three buildings for the University of Denver, the old Central Presbyterian Church, Trinity Methodist Church, the beautiful First Presbyterian Church in Colorado Springs, and his most nostalgic building, the Central City Opera House. Almost all of these buildings stand today— Roeschlaub's buildings were constructed for stable institutions and, except for Trinity Methodist Church, none of them is today very close to the fast-changing center of Denver.

Early Buildings:
Ashland School, Central Presbyterian
Church, and the Central City Opera House

Although Roeschlaub's career in the 1870's must have been successful, little is known of it. His office was listed in Denver's first telephone directory (1879) as being at the south corner of 15th and Larimer Streets. Only three buildings which date from the 1870's are attributable to Roeschlaub— the Ashland School of 1874, the second building for the Central Presbyterian Church of 1876, and the famous Central City Opera House of 1878.[3] The three demonstrate considerable stylistic discontinuity. The Ashland School has complex massing, a Second Empire character, a barn-like gable at the end of one wing, and a more standard triangular gable at the end of the other. The brickwork is characteristicly early Roeschlaub: very tightly laid red

Robert Roeschlaub/Peter Gottesleben house, 1889–demolished.

Robert Roeschlaub/South facade, Chamberlin Observatory, 1889.

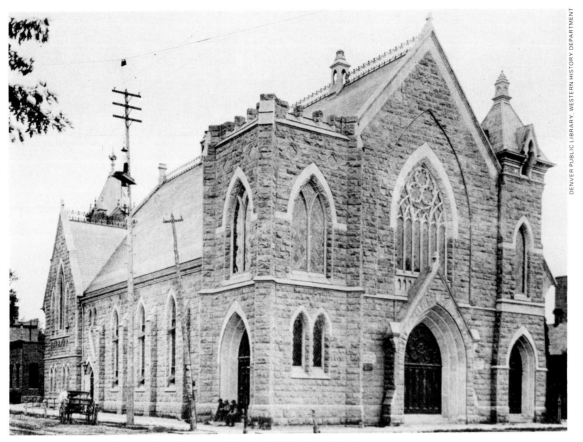

Robert Roeschlaub/Central Presbyterian Church, 1876–demolished.

brick with crisp white mortar. The school relates to the tradition of schoolhouse architecture in which a rigorous separation of boys and girls is expressed by generally contrasting wings spreading laterally from an authoritative central area. Although this separation of the sexes was maintained for several decades in the Denver Public Schools, it was never expressed architecturally with such clarity again.

The second building for the Central Presbyterian Church, used until 1892 when Edbrooke's larger church was finished, was completed in 1876 at a cost of about $50,000. The church shows considerable influence from English High Victorian Gothic churches. Its roof was properly polychromed, a common practice in Denver, and the general character of Roeschlaub's sketches of the building is similar to that of an English parish church. Roeschlaub did not, however, accept his model whole-heartedly and the church can only be seen as a provincial variant on the model. The "gothic spire," never built for lack of funds, was to have been balanced by a small tower with an almost Second Empire roof; the details were so hard and precise that they related more easily to the early gothic revival than they did to the High Victorian Gothic, and the massing was so staunchly rectilinear and constrained that there was little "picturesque" about it. In short, Roeschlaub's church was an amalgamation of styles and approaches to architecture. It was clearly a young man's building, and

had little of the sophistication and subtlety which are so evident in later buildings by the architect.

The Central City Opera House is undoubtedly Roeschlaub's best known building. Its austere stone facade gives the smallish building a sobriety and grandness lacking in most buildings of the Second Empire style. Probably for budgetary reasons, Roeschlaub eschewed the opportunity to cover the building in ornament. He divided the facade into three blocky masses, a central area with a mansard roof flanked by two towers, and succeeded in giving the building a great deal more solidity and depth than its neighboring street buildings with their implacably flat facades. The Central City Opera House is admirable for its straightforwardness and simplicity. There is little waste, and the whole building has a tightness of execution typical of Roeschlaub's best buildings.

The Opera House is important in Roeschlaub's career as the first building in which he began to analyze, break apart, and redesign human movement. The complex machination of staircases and doorways in the little building anticipated his later architecture such as Trinity Methodist-Episcopal Church, University Hall, and the schools of the later eighties and the early nineties. All of these buildings share a tendency to avoid the grand entrance, to divide movement into manageable steps, and to devote a great deal of space to staircases, hallways, and foyers.

Robert Roeschlaub/Central City Opera House,
Central City, 1878.

Schools

Among Roeschlaub's most successful buildings are the small schools which he built in the early 1880's. Many of these buildings still stand in something close to their original form, paradigms of good, economical, tight architecture. They share a compactness and simplicity with the Central City Opera House, although their detail and brick execution are more similar to the Ashland School of 1874.

The first of these schools, the Ebert School, was built in 1880 on the corner of 22nd and Logan Streets. Later expanded by the architect himself into a much larger and more complex building, the original scheme was a vaguely Second Empire cube built of brick, stone, and metal. It was a spare, basic building, its restrained brick cornice harking back to Denver's commercial architecture of the early 1860's. The brick was laid as in the Ashland School, in simple planes with distinct edges. The white mortar made each brick stand out in precise relief, giving the building a solidly constructed appearance. The central towers were pulled into the building mass, and the roof was detailed in metal with clean, repetitive vertical lines. The whole facade was further corseted by horizontal banding of contrasting smooth-cut stone around the first floor. The plane of the building was firmly established and nothing was allowed to disrupt it in any important way. Indeed, the building was most symbolic of the constraint and propriety of Denver's educational system in the 1880's, representing a view of public institutions in which economy and solidity were the primary values.

Ebert School was a great success for Roeschlaub, and he designed schools for the Denver Public School system throughout the 1880's. The first few, Gilpin School of 1881, Longfellow School of 1882, and Whittier School of 1883, were variations on a familiar theme: all were built of brick with white mortar and white stone trim, all were characterized by a solidity and geometry, and each was, like the Ebert School, a small and finely wrought masterpiece of institutional architecture. These four buildings set Roeschlaub apart as Denver's leading institutional architect, an architect whose vision was clean and hard when compared to that of Frank E. Edbrooke in the same years. It is evident that Edbrooke's architecture was affected by these brilliant little schools of Roeschlaub. Even a cursory look at the First Baptist Church of 1883 shows that the brick is similarly detailed and the use of rather planar, contrasting color ornament seems clearly related to the Roeschlaub buildings of 1880, 1881, and 1882 in spite of the Tabor-like exuberance of the church.

Robert Roeschlaub/Ebert School, 1880—demolished.

Robert Roeschlaub/Denver City High School designed in 1881. West wing constructed in 1881 and the building completed in 1889.

Roeschlaub's most ambitious and important early building was the high school for District Number 1, later known as Old East High School. This building, sited on an entire city block and surrounded by a park-like garden, was designed to consist of a central three-story building flanked by two smaller and symmetrically disposed pavilions. It was built in two stages. The first of the small side pavilions was completed in 1881, but the central area and the other pavilion were not completed until 1889. The program for the project was lavish, and the high school was obviously intended as an important civic monument in nineteenth century Denver. The side pavilions clearly related to Roeschlaub's small schools of the early 1880's, but the treatment was much more generous, resulting in a more official, expensive, and ceremonial look for the building.

Robert Roeschlaub/Denver City High School (interior), designed 1881, built in 1881 and 1889.

As an architectural monument, the high school was certainly less successful than Roeschlaub's smaller buildings of the same years. Its detail seemed overly finicky and the windows were crowded with a repetitive energy onto the surface. However, the central entrance pavilion was grand in spite of the crowding of details. The entrance arch was wide and the stairs rushed impressively up inside the building mass, and the interior was a marvel which could never have survived today's fire inspection. The halls pushed up the full height of the building, detailed almost exclusively in wood. Skylights filtered natural light down into the rooms and along the many staircases and high-ceilinged galleries. As in the Central City Opera House, Roeschlaub was obsessed with movement. Going between classes and entering the library were more important to him than actually being anywhere within the building, and he glorified the staircases and hallways, inviting movement throughout this great High Victorian palace of learning.

Roeschlaub's tendency toward a kind of eclecticism, a tendency which was not quite present in his early school architecture, emerged strongly in 1884 when he designed the notable Emerson School which still stands at the corner of 14th and Ogden Streets. This school was clearly a transition building in Roeschlaub's career. It began his movement toward the massively roofed structure which dominated his work as the decade continued, and it signaled the beginning of the dark brick buildings which he designed almost exclusively throughout the 1880's. Light stone trim is almost unused in the Emerson School. Instead, ornamental work is done in brick with dark mortar to differentiate it from the light-mortared brick of the structural walls. This dark ornamental banding cuts across the facade decreasing the contrast in the building and unifying it. Stylistically, Emerson School is a strange building. The entrance pavilion is clearly derived from an ecclesiastical source, giving a "churchy" rather than institutional effect. A formal Renaissance brick arch flanked by a pair of symmetrical windows is juxtaposed against the informal porch, and the entire composition seems to be a wedding of church and state.

Symbolism in the school is given a new twist by the presence of a very large and very formal sundial on the facade. This feature became increasingly popular in domestic architecture as the century proceeded, but its use on Emerson School was unique in the history of nineteenth century Denver school architecture. The

Robert Roeschlaub/Emerson School, 1420 Ogden, 1884.

sundial is detailed in the same neo-Renaissance manner as the arched entrance and is treated as an antiphonal shape on the facade. It assumes its place authoritatively on an otherwise empty wall. Bands from the windows cut through it without violating its shape, and it serves to connect the first and second floors. Above the sundial and within the arch itself is the name of the school. The entire form seems a firm reminder to the student to be on time.

Examined in detail, the Emerson School is one of Roeschlaub's most successful and most beautiful buildings. Its condition today, while not really bad in the structural sense, demonstrates a modern misunderstanding of the building as a whole. The trim, which originally matched the dark brick, is now very light and devisive, making the windows overly assertive and separating the roof from the building itself. The construction of ugly outbuildings off the main facade further distracts the viewers attention from the major compositional elements— the portal, the windows and the sundial. Small metal roofs formerly topped the chimneys, making them appear to be castle-like towers. These are now gone, and the chimneys are nothing but chimneys.

Robert Roeschlaub/Entrance detail, Emerson School, 1420 Ogden, 1884.

Robert Roeschlaub/Emerson School, 1420 Ogden, 1884.

Robert Roeschlaub/Hyde Park School, 1889.

Roeschlaub's buildings for the University of Denver and School District Number 1 form as clear and inter-related a group as did his schools of the early eighties. They are characterized by huge, billowing roofs, Richardsonian brick arches, square towers with onion domes, and extensive terra cotta ornamentation. They can be viewed in strict contrast to the earlier buildings in their complexity, lavishness, and size. Commissioned by officials who spared no expense, the buildings seem to advance toward the viewer— towers, chimneys and gables push out from the basic rectangle and stand in defiance of the enormous shingled expanse of the roof.

The first of these buildings was the Hyde Park School, built in 1887 at the corner of 36th and Gilpin Streets. The building still stands in reasonably good condition and has been renamed Wyatt School. Stylistically and formally complex, the Hyde Park School uses its corner site to great advantage. The roof and the corner tower are canted at a forty-five degree angle to the clock and align themselves to face the corner. The other two facades of the building on the street fronts are not so strongly emphasized and lack the dominating tower which signals the main entrance. The style of the building is best termed Richardsonian, although it does not derive from any particular building in Richardson's career. The onion domed tower, however, is anything but Richardsonian and seems to relate to the tradition of corner-towered domestic architecture more than to institutional design. It is notable for its wit and

lightness, and the subtle curves of its profile relate happily to the rounded arches below.

Hyde Park School is notable in Roeschlaub's career for its lack of symmetry and its resultant rambling, disconnected quality. The parts in this school overshadow the whole in spite of the expansive roof which aids in unifying the composition. Gables, chimney, and towers form a picturesque fence around the roofed structure, standing in a line with little tectonic inter-relationship and almost no logical ordering.

Roeschlaub seems to have recognized both the strengths and the weaknesses of Hyde Park School, for his next two school buildings were more tightly ordered. The Corona School of 1889, now called the Dora Moore School, and the Wyman School of 1890 both use the same formal vocabulary as the Hyde Park School, but with the addition of a more clearly organized and symmetrical plan. The Corona School, between 8th and 9th on Corona Street, is an extremely unified building which uses the corner entrance which the architect tried at the Hyde Park School on all four corners of the building. The result is a balance of the tension of the towers which pull away from the center of the building. The enormous roof which so fascinated Roeschlaub in the later eighties is simplified and organized in the Corona School. It is not a rambling and inexplicable mass which totally dominates the building as in the earlier Hyde Park School. It is reduced and clarified into a comprehensible covering for this complicated and beautifully planned school.

Robert Roeschlaub/Corner tower, Wyman School, 1630 Williams, 1890.

Robert Roeschlaub/Terra cotta sign, Wyman School, 1630 Williams, 1890.

Robert Roeschlaub/Wyman School, 1630 Williams, 1890.

Robert Roeschlaub/Facade detail, Wyman School, 1630 Williams, 1890.

Robert Roeschlaub/Entrance arch, Wyman School, 1630 Williams, 1890.

The most exciting and notable feature of the Corona School is its expensive and beautifully detailed terra cotta. Most of the detail in the building is natural in inspiration. Roeschlaub shared an interest in vegetable or plant detail with Richardson and the Richardsonian architects. The bulk of the ornament, however, is not Richardsonian in character, but comes from the acanthas decoration used in Roman architecture, the Renaissance, and Baroque design. The loose, swirling rhythm of the acanthus leaves was used for banding, around the entrance arches, and in the gables, giving the building an elegance which it otherwise lacks and underscoring the classicism of the Romanesque arches.

Robert Roeschlaub/Corona School, 846 Corona, 1889.

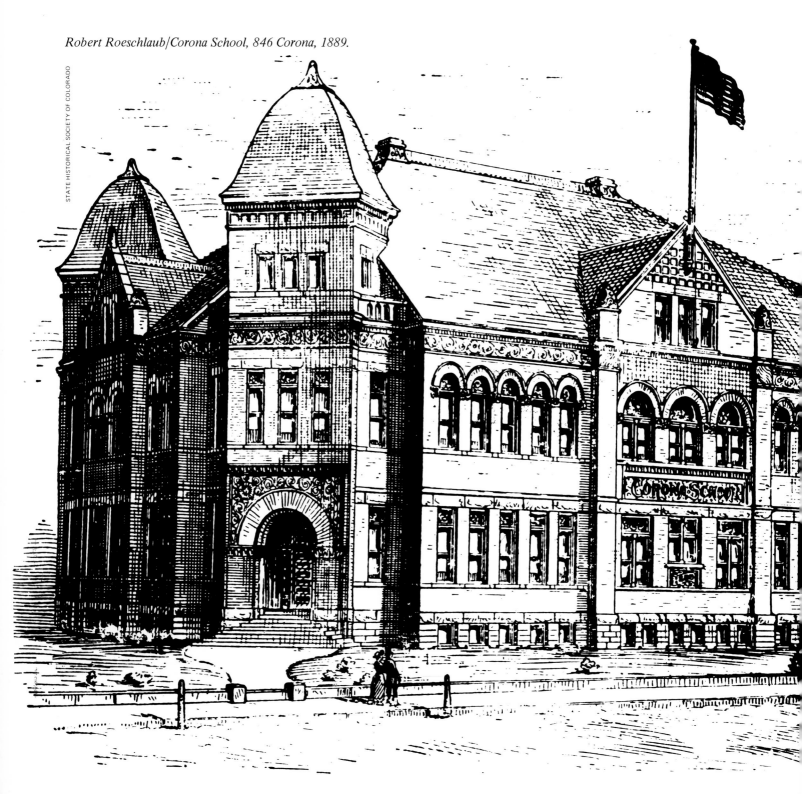

Robert Roeschlaub/Facade detail, Corona School, 846 Corona, 1889.

Robert Roeschlaub/Facade detail, Corona School, 846 Corona, 1889.

Robert Roeschlaub/Entrance detail, Corona School, 846 Corona, 1889.

Robert Roeschlaub/Gable detail, Corona School, 846 Corona, 1889.

The Corona School and its sister buildings, the enlarged Ebert School and University Hall for the University of Denver, all exhibit the same formal arrangement, large symmetrical facades with entrance at the corner and peaked roofs. All three buildings show Roeschlaub's fascination with movement and circulation within the building. Corner entrances all feed into a large central area (which has often not survived the rigors of modern fire inspection), and movement is then diffused into many staircases.

Robert Roeschlaub/Ebert School (after enlargement), 1890.

The continual movement toward and then away from the center of the building succeeded in unifying Roeschlaub's later architecture. The buildings like the later Ebert School and University Hall are radially symmetrical rather than symmetrical along each facade, and thus can be comprehended at a glance. The visitor can see where he is expected to enter; upon entrance, he knows to go to the center of the building and from there can see the staircase which will take him to the part of the building to which he wants to go.[4]

Roeschlaub's fascination with circulation and movement is a key explanation of the formal complexity of his mature designs. The facade of the University Hall building pulls in and pushes out simultaneously. The act of rising is clearly expressed in the diagonally massed staircase towers with their staggered windows. Multiple entrances enable the student or faculty member to enter from any part of the campus. University Hall and Roeschlaub's schools of the later eighties were buildings intended to be the centers of their respective communities. They related to their environment in multiple directions and seldom had a "preferred" point of view. They are almost archetypally democratic buildings, buildings for a great many people.

Robert Roeschlaub/University Hall, Denver University, 2199 South University Boulevard, 1890.

Robert Roeschlaub/Stair tower, University Hall, Denver University, 1890.

Robert Roeschlaub/University Hall, Denver University, 1890.

Robert Roeschlaub/Column and capital, Main entry, University Hall, Denver University, 1890.

Robert Roeschlaub/Entrance, University Hall, Denver University, 1890.

Robert Roeschlaub/Union Block, 1882–demolished.

Commercial Architecture:
the King Block, the Times Building, and the Union Block

Roeschlaub's commercial architecture of the early eighties is remarkable in being almost totally unlike his institutional architecture of the same period. The three notable buildings– the King Block of 1882, the Times Building of 1881, and the Union Block of 1882– are considerably more complex, exuberant, and stylistically confusing than the schools.

The King Block, where Roeschlaub kept his offices after its completion in 1883, was a three-story stone street block enlarged several years later (by Roeschlaub) to become a four and one-half story block with a mansard roof. Originally the building consisted of five equal bays with a very small entrance bay and a large signboard at the top. The detailing was erratic and finicky. Small triangles topped the windows on the third floor, and the second floor featured raised gothic arches on the center two of the four windows in each bay. The effect was punctuated, nervous, and exciting, quite unlike the contained and sober Ebert School. Enlargement did little to simplify the building. The mansard roof was interrupted frequently with spiky dormers which intensified the episodic quality of the building.

The Times Building, which was begun in 1881, was built to house the *Denver Times* and stood at 1547-1551 Lawrence Street. Its three-bay facade was more symmetrical than the facade of the King Block and was a successful and active commercial facade. Its three

stories were raised from the street in an arrangement later borrowed by Edbrooke in his Chamber of Commerce Building. The stone was smooth-cut and was given a strong, vital surface relief by the design of the building. Roeschlaub followed the paradigm of the Renaissance palazzo in the building's tendency to become more complex and elaborate with each progressive floor. The raised basement was absolutely unornamented. The first floor was austere and simple. The second floor exhibited roundels, composite capitals, and notched segmental arches, and the third floor had stumpy columns, small segmental arches, an arch of triumph, and a large, heavy cornice.

The facade of the Times Building was probably the most sophisticated and exciting constructed in Denver up to that year, including the Tabor buildings by the Edbrookes. It was confident, beautifully articulated, and expressive of the strength and urbanity of the press. Its presence in 1881 was surely as important as the presence of Roeschlaub's very different Ebert School. Taken together, the buildings are exemplary of the architect's extraordinary powers and versatility, especially in designing a building keyed to its specific program.

The Union Block, constructed in 1882 to house the Union Bank, Gottesleben's Jewelry Store, and the *Denver Tribune,* was weaker and more difficult than the

Times Building. Its program was complex; the single block was required to express clearly three different tenants. Its efforts to do so were not entirely unsuccessful, but the unity of the project suffered somewhat.

The Union Block was a three-story business block constructed of stone which was rather heavily rusticated for its date. Its detailing was both High Victorian and Second Empire. The small cupola which defined the top of the bank was similar to the shorter tower of the old Central Presbyterian Church. The ornamental gable which stood above Peter Gottesleben's Jewelry Store was more High Victorian in character in spite of its mansard roof. Taken together, the building was loose and undefined in spite of the massive character of its material, and it remained one of Denver's least distinguished building blocks.

Trinity Church

Roeschlaub's survival during the slump of the mid-eighties was fortunate.[5] The first major building which came from his office after 1885 is, perhaps, his greatest. The Trinity Methodist-Episcopal Church (the word Episcopal, which was carved into the sign of the church in 1887, has now been filled in) is Roeschlaub's most visible building. It stands across Broadway from Edbrooke's masterpiece, the Brown Hotel, and the two buildings are today the most significant survivals from the greatest building boom in the history of Denver. The stone of the building, which had darkened to a characterless gray, was cleaned in 1964 to reveal a native rhyolite, a volcanic granite from Castle Rock. The stone is light beige with hints of red and blue and the subtle glitter of mica. It was quarried in rusticated blocks of varying heights and laid in distinct and attractive horizontal bands which help give the building a grounded look in spite of its pointed gables and tall, dramatic tower. The massing of the church as well as its plan clearly derive from Richardsonian sources. Indeed, Roeschlaub's Trinity Church seems to be a gothic compaction of Richardson's Trinity Church in Boston, completed in 1876. Windows are grouped similarly, and the stone is laid with a comparable grandeur and strength. The forms of the nave, exaggerated transcept, corner towers, and outbuildings huddle together to form

From left to right: Trinity Church by Robert Roeschlaub, the Metropole Hotel by Frank E. Edbrooke, and the Brown Hotel by Frank E. Edbrooke, Broadway and 18th Streets. Circa 1892.

a single composition grouped massively around the defining corner spire. The tower, sited among very tall buildings since the early nineties, has always seemed to struggle for its height. Its solidity and resolute stoniness make imagery of weight vie with imagery of height, and Trinity tower is among the most active towers in Denver. The two other corner towers cling protectively to the church itself and the drama of the corner tower is singular. Because the church stands at the nexus of Denver's grids, the tower can be seen from a great many vantage points— a stabilizing form in the confusion of modern downtown.

Entering Trinity Church is similar to entering the Central City Opera House. Three identical entrance portals separate the worshipers into three paths. From the small, undramatic entrance space, four staircases lead to the sanctuary, two in the corner towers and two under the gable. The worshiper moves up the stairs with little preparation for the grandness of the sanctuary itself. In spite of its flat roof the interior is awesome in

Robert Roeschlaub/Tower detail, Trinity Methodist Church, 1820 Broadway, 1887.

Robert Roeschlaub/Trinity Methodist Church, 1820 Broadway, 1887.

scale and its fascinating details. The windows give the light warm earthy tones, and the entire room glows with a golden hue. The overall effect is encompassing, maternal, and protective; the sanctuary is capacious rather than dramatic.

Trinity Church is confident and impressive, difficult to discuss because of its sheer beauty and quality. The drawings for the church, which still survive in the archives of Fuller and Fuller, Roeschlaub's successor firm, are notable for their careful detail. Roeschlaub was probably the best draftsman of nineteenth century Denver, and his drawings show a probity and concentration lacking in the more workaday plans of Edbrooke which survive in the State Historical Society. The drawings for Trinity Church were done in pen and ink with infill of watercolor even for the renditions of the roof trussing, metal work, and pews. Attention to detail is fantastic. Roeschlaub's conception of a building must be seen in direct opposition to Edbrooke's. For Roeschlaub, a building was put together from separately designed elements rather than conceived as a whole. Roeschlaub's eye moved everywhere; there are drawings

Robert Roeschlaub/Window detail, Trinity Methodist Church, 1820 Broadway, 1887.

Robert Roeschlaub/Tower detail Trinity
Methodist Church, 1820 Broadway, 1887.

Robert Roeschlaub/Window detail, Trinity Methodist Church, 1820 Broadway, 1887.

Robert Roeschlaub/Facade detail, Trinity Methodist Church, 1820 Broadway, 1887.

of the side of a pew and the carving around the organ, drawings of the iron gateways, the banisters, the laid stone at the base of the tower, the entrance, the complex wooden rafters which spring from the side walls and from which the interior ceiling is suspended. In short, there are drawings of every detail within the building. Roeschlaub did not conceive of a building in plan and elevation as did Edbrooke and as did most architects of the later nineteenth century. Rather, he conceived of a building as an incredibly complex aggregation of forms which were congealed into an active and detailed whole. The finished watercolor of the whole church came at the end of an enormously concentrated and difficult design period, and must be seen in light of the drawings for every detail of the buildings.

This concentration and detail planning contrast sharply with the Central Presbyterian Church designed a few years later by Frank E. Edbrooke. Trinity Church had a very high budget— $200,000 compared to the more modest $150,000 for the larger Central Church. Trinity is complex, compact, and chunky; Central Church is large, schematic, and simple. Trinity is characterized by a profusion of detail concentrated into a rather small form. Central Church is full of air and room, with the details diffused throughout the building and little of the urgency and formal restlessness which are so evident in Roeschlaub's building.

Roeschlaub almost never built buildings which are based directly on a prototype of the past or in the architecture reproduced in the national architectural magazines. Rather, his buildings were always original and almost always very fresh. He examined his programs in detail, and his surviving drawings evidence a restless, relentless mind which probed into every aspect of architecture regardless of its character or scale. In many ways, his buildings were old-fashioned and concerned with detail, complexity, and diversity. He did not participate very fully in the trends to simplify and unify architecture regardless of its character or scale. While he did participate in the rather broad American Richardsonianism of the 1880's, he did not do so fully. His massing schemes were often far more complex and subtle than Richardson's own.

Roeschlaub was recognized as the leading architect of Denver by his colleagues when they established the Colorado Chapter of the American Institute of Architects in 1891— he was the first president of that organization and was unanimously elected to that office every year between 1891 and 1911. He was the first licensed architect in Colorado and the first good architect to come to the state. He was not a slap-dash architect, an architect of the boom. His buildings were solid, secure, and expensive. His architecture carried through the entire history of significant Denver architecture in the nineteenth century, and his few bad or confused buildings are outnumbered by his good ones. Although Roeschlaub did not have the importance and success of Frank E. Edbrooke or the sheer formal skill of William Lang, he produced a confident and often exciting body of architecture in the nineteenth century.

Robert Roeschlaub/Trinity Methodist Church, 1820 Broadway, watercolor by the architect, 1887.

ꞋEclecticism

Complex Provincial Architecture
during the late *1880's*

As a critical concept, eclecticism is not without difficulties. Is a building appropriately and intelligently eclectic or is it slap-dash and ignorant? Can an architect who works in a single style be called an eclectic because his buildings exhibit eclectic features within the single style? An architectural firm like Varian and Sterner designed buildings which, while internally eclectic, can nevertheless be classified as "Richardsonian Romanesque" with a high degree of accuracy and consistency.[1] Other local architects, like the Baerresen brothers or J.J. Huddart, designed Richardsonian buildings, late Second Empire buildings, High

Victorian "Gothic" buildings, and often buildings with Moorish, Renaissance, and neo-classical details, making them eclectic in the most exaggerated sense of the word. Their careers were not marked by a desire for consistency and order. They did not possess anything approximating an "architectural philosophy" and seemed to be architects who took full and serious advantage of the building boom.

Denver could have been called, in the nineteenth century, an eclectic city. Composed of men who came from all over the world for a variety of reasons, Denver possessed a diverse and often eccentric clientele to which the architectural profession had to cater. Men like Frank E. Edbrooke had a unique ability to shape people's dreams into the dominant modes of American architecture, but lesser architects had considerable difficulty with their clients. Edbrooke apparently built no Queen Anne houses after 1890. He built only advanced architecture and did not mold his architectural sensibilities to fit his clients' old-fashioned dreams. He kept abreast of national taste and, in so doing, gave Denver a very advanced general appearance. Other architects— Huddart, Quayle, Stuckert, Balcomb and Rice, the Baerresen brothers, and Franklin Kidder— altered their styles to fit the client, the building program, and, often, their own whim. Their careers had complex, often unpredictable shapes— an advanced or up-to-date building might be designed at the same time as three or four inexplicably retardataire buildings. A building exhibiting great stylistic purity might have come from the same office in the same month as several buildings with almost no stylistic consistency.

The essential eclecticism of civilization in the American west has already been noted. Based fundamentally on a masculine pioneer image, the cities of the west maintained their desire for virile and direct action until the great crash of 1893. The addition of the "health spa" and the resort to the imagery of Denver altered this impetuous and excessive life-style with new restraints— conformity, exercise, sobriety, and respectability. Men who came to make quick fortunes in the most ruthless possible manner mingled with men who came to spend a sedate and quite life-time with their families in the Rockies. Men from Europe, from the east, from the middle-west, from the far west, and from the great nomadic nowhere of the mountains co-existed within the same city and competed in the massive rush to make Denver into their kind of town. The desire for haste came face to face with the desire for permanence, and the city of Denver as we know it today came into being with extraordinary speed in the most confusing and eclectic period in its history.

Most of the architects of the city in the late eighties and early nineties succumbed to the confusion of their times and designed extraordinarily diverse buildings.

...hitect Unknown/Colonel Dodge residence, 12th and Pennsylvania,
...een Anne, High Victorian, chateau, Richardsonian, and neo-classical features, 1889.

Architect Unknown/Residence, 1410 Elizabeth. This home demonstrates a decorative or surface eclecticism which differs greatly from the more studied eclecticism of William Lang. The architect in this case has added various decorative styles to the basic Queen Anne street house which was very common in Denver by the mid to late 1880's. Circa 1888-89.

Architect Unknown/Bracket and cornice detail, residence, 1410 Elizabeth, circa 1888-89.

PHOTO: EDWARDS AND BROWN

Architect Unknown/Detail along the eave, residence, 1647 Emerson, circa 1889.

PHOTO: EDWARDS AND BROWN

125

Architect Unknown/Residence, 1647 Emerson. This house has the traditional amalgam of Queen Anne, neo-classical, and Richardsonian details which is so common in Denver architecture of the 1880's. The antique past, the English ancestral home, and the new American style are all evoked in these memorable dwellings. Circa 1889.

Architect Unknown/Residence, 1600 Emerson. One of the best of the surviving houses on Capitol Hill, this residence is too fussy to be by Lang. Its facade bristles with life, but a life contained by the insistent rectangle of the plan and the rusticated stone corseting. Circa 1889.

Architect Unknown (Possibly William Lang)/Three middle class dwellings. These three houses are ample display of the essential similarity in design, massing, and detailing of Denver's homes. Middle class and lower middle class dwellings were generally miniaturized (as opposed to simplified) dwellings and were extremely similar to the dwellings for the upper classes. Circa 1889.

Architect Unknown/Flat apartments, 2355-2361 Ogden. Among the most eclectic surviving terraces in Denver. These apartments are Richardsonian, Shingle Style, and neo-Renaissance. Circa 1890.

The Baerresen brothers concocted the High Victorian pile of the old St. Joseph's hospital as well as the relatively schematic and Richardsonian facade of the Mack Building. Franklin Kidder designed a Richardsonian masterpiece, the Asbury Methodist Church, while he was finishing construction on the rusticated gothic Christ Methodist Church. J.J. Huddart built the Langian stone Creswell House at 1244 Grant in the same year as he built the Ruskinian Kinneavy Terrace at 27th and Stout. Examples of this eclecticism within a career (as opposed to eclecticism within a building) abound, as the majority of Denver's architects intentionally avoided consistency within their careers. They did not design their buildings with their biographers in mind and left architectural legacies which are not critically comprehensible in any easy terms.

John J. Huddart

J.J. Huddart, one of the most talented architects in the city during the nineteenth century, was born in England on August 25, 1857, at the height of the High Victorian Gothic period. His bent was not aesthetic and he was educated at a London engineering school.[2] Huddart left England in 1880 to seek his fortune abroad. He is recorded as having been in Brazil until 1881 and in Australia until sometime in 1881. In that year or early in 1882, Huddart came to the United States and practiced briefly in Jacksonville, Florida.[3] "Being ambitious and full of energy, he soon perceived that the west offered the best opportunities for the young man willing to hustle and do hard work."[4] After his arrival in Denver he worked in Edbrooke's office as a draftsman between 1882 and 1888. He has been called chief-draftsman as his name is associated with several of Edbrooke's most important buildings, including the Cooper Building, the Ernest and Cranmer Building, and the Quincy Building. While the commercial structures from his own office show slight influence from the Edbrookian years, he seems to have been a decidedly more High Victorian architect whose preferences were for polychromy, a diversity of materials within one building, and rather picturesque facades. The modern viewer must make a great imaginative leap to say that the designer of Kinneavy Terrace and the designer of the Ernest and Cranmer Building were the same man. It is more likely that Edbrooke used Huddart's engineering skills in those early years of his practice; Huddart was probably never Edbrooke's "chief-designer," if there ever was such a post in Edbrooke's office. He designed slightly Edbrookian commercial structures like the Bank Block, where he kept his offices until his death in 1930, but the majority of his buildings were eclectic and rather picturesque.

The Kinneavy Terrace, still standing at the corner of 27th and Stout Streets, was designed by Huddart in 1888 or early in 1889. Its episodic facade is a stylistic combination of elements derived from Chicago commercial structures via Edbrooke, High Victorian architecture in England, and the Queen Anne style house. The pointed gables with their rounded arches and rather stumpy corner towers are decidedly Chicago style; the polychrome bands of the stone and the patterning of the tiles in the false roof are English, and the wooden porches and corner tower derive from Queen Anne houses. The associations are complex and do not seem to be strictly appropriate. There is no particular reason why a terraced apartment building should have imagery from an English church or from a commercial structure. Queen Anne seems to be more appropriate to a domestic structure, but even its most characteristic features— the paneled gable and half-timbering— are omitted from Kinneavy Terrace. Given this stylistic confusion, it is easy to dismiss the structure as inappropriate and discount the validity of the building. This dismissal is neither fair nor intelligent. The building is clearly and self-consciously eclectic, and there is no formal reason to assume that Huddart did not knowingly and intentionally create this odd mixture of styles. Kinneavy Terrace, in spite of its stylistic dependence on past architecture, is decidedly modern in that it uses past architecture with little regard for original or historical conventions. It is a building which considers nothing from the history of architecture as sacred and which speaks of the modern architect's role as composer of all that is best from the past.

Yet, Huddart's use of eclectic detailing and massing was eclectic in itself. Rarely do we find buildings which use the architecture of the past or from the immediate era in the same way. The Creswell house, for example, is decidedly unlike the Kinneavy Terrace in its internal eclecticism. It makes slight use of the Queen Anne house with a great deal of Richardsonian detail and there is very little of the English High Victorian in it. The treatment of windows on the north facade is both original and exciting. The most important and immediate influence discernable in this small street house is that of William Lang's even more original (but better built) houses of the same year, 1889, like the Everts residence. The Creswell residence seems to have been one of the most Langian building of Huddart's career. He was quite proud of it; he used his own drawing of the front hall in his advertisements.

John J. Huddart/Kinneavy Terrace, 1889, 27th and Stout.

John J. Huddart/Creswell house, 1244 Grant, 1889.

John J. Huddart/Staircase hall, Creswell residence, 1244 Grant.
Photograph published in the Western Architect and Building News.
Vol. 1, No. 10, 1889.

John J. Huddart/Window detail, main facade, Creswell house, 1244 Grant, 1899.

John J. Huddart/Front porch, Creswell house, 1244 Grant, 1889.

131

John J. Huddart/Athelston Apartments, 1890—demolished.

William Lang probably provided the influence for two other Huddart buildings, the Athelston Apartments and the Cole Lyden residence. The Athelston was perhaps the most exciting terrace apartment building of its time. Its actively rusticated stone facade was composed in interconnecting towers and pavilions whose curved walls and roofs swelled with internal volume. The detail was Richardsonian, but the massing and the roof silhouette were High Victorian if not Second Empire. This house seems almost to be Huddart's challenge to Lang's powers as a stylistic amalgamator, and it is perhaps the only building by a Denver architect which succeeds in the challenge. The house is Shingle Style, Richardsonian, Queen Anne, Dutch, and neo-Renaissance. Its Dutch end gables relate directly to Lang's Washington Street townhouses. Lacking the formal brilliance of Lang's buildings, it nevertheless has some virtuoso features such as the double-functioning keystone and balcony support which may derive from the Everts house, although precise dating of the two monuments is not possible.

Other and probably later buildings by Huddart, such as the McClair Apartments, are more decidedly Richardsonian and lack the multiple or Langian eclecticism apparent in the Athelston, Kinneavy Terrace, the Creswell house, and the Lyden residence. The clarity, symmetry, and tightness of the McClair terrace apartment is not unique in Huddart's career, and the series of buildings which relate to it probably form a group which dates between 1890 and 1893. The William L. Stephens house and the Mrs. M. Kittredge house are both examples of this rather hardened Richardsonianism. Its use of chateauesque features, flattened and simplified in the manner of Richardson's very late houses, is the hallmark of this single stylistic chord from Huddart's very diverse career. These buildings can be compared favorably to Edbrooke's later houses. They are almost as simple, but their proportions are more delicate and their detailing is more subtle and less forboding.

John J. Huddart/Cole Lyden residence, 1890—demolished.

John J. Huddart (?)/Roof detail, terrace, 625 East 16th Street, circa 1890.

John J. Huddart (?)/Terrace, 625 East 16th Street, circa 1890.

133

John J. Huddart/McClair Apartments, 1892–demolished.

John J. Huddart/Mrs. William Stephens house, 1891–demolished.

Huddart's attempt to simplify and unify the sources of his architecture indicates his ultimate concern with local success and his belief in the submission of the architect to his milieu. Huddart, unlike William Lang, did not allow the continuation of an outdated eclecticism to ruin a distinguished career as a Denver architect. His architecture of the 1880's was of the grab-bag variety; it was loose, often exuberant, and based on the single principle operative in such a city as Denver by such an architect as Huddart— saleability and client pleasure.

Huddart's career was very well reviewed by the *Western Architect and Building News.* The journal published more photographs of his buildings than of buildings by any other local architect, including Edbrooke. The reason for this popularity in the media is not given, but it may relate to Huddart's great personal charm and his ability to conform his architecture to a specific program. This attitude toward architecture is rarely praised by historians, who prefer what they might consider to be more ultimately important principles. Nevertheless it assures professional success to the competent and thoughtful architect. The buildings themselves are not full of brilliance and novelty, but they are often very accurate indicators of their own times— more accurate in some ways than the buildings of a consistent and principled architect like Edbrooke or Lang. J.J. Huddart's career reflects the hegemony of

Denver in the 1880's. Further, it expresses the hegemony of the Rocky Mountain west in the 1880's, for Huddart's career was not, like Edbrooke's or Lang's, predominantly local. He designed the four-story Swift Building in Pueblo, the Gus Holmes Building in Salt Lake City, the American National Bank in Leadville, the

Adams County Court house, the Bank of Montrose, and schools in Englewood and Durango. His career was not overwhelmingly successful (his only offices were in Denver), but it was notable. His buildings fulfilled the taste of their times with an eclectic efficiency and as in the case of the McClair Apartments, with grace.

John J. Huddart/The Bank Block, 1889—demolished.

John J. Huddart/The Swift Building, Pueblo, Colorado, 1890.

Franklin Kidder

Franklin Kidder's career shows considerably more restraint than that of Huddart. A tubercular, he moved to Denver in 1888 for his health. His life was extremely regimented and spartan; he slept out of doors in a tent and rode his bicycle to work daily from his home at 26th and Federal in the Highlands to his office at 14th and California. Kidder's superior training and his undeniable pedantry placed him at the front of his profession in Denver. His office was unique in being advertised by a huge sign on the roof of the building, and he was listed in the *Denver Directory* as a "consulting architect" as well as a practicing architect. His best buildings were churches and houses, although he did design several small buildings for commercial purposes and supervised the remodeling of the Broadway Hotel. His parsonage for the Central Presbyterian Church, designed late in 1889, had the distinction of being the only building by a Denver architect ever published in a national architectural magazine.[5]

Kidder's buildings in Denver are not as eclectic as Huddart's, but neither are they stylistically consistent.

His predominant mode of planning was a somewhat free Richardsonianism. He made attempts, however, at designing other styles, and his most stylistically disparate building was the Christ Methodist-Episcopal Church, designed late in 1889 and still standing on the corner of 22nd and Ogden Streets. This church reflects almost no Richardsonian influence and seems to be an attempt on Kidder's part to build a church using in modified form the principles of the ecclesiologists in England. The windows in the church are gothic, and a pointed corner tower was used rather than the squatter Richardsonian tower which Kidder used in churches like the more notable Asbury Methodist Church. Entrance to the church school and offices is through a low-roofed porch which, in the symbolism of the ecclesiologists, was intended to make the viewer feel humble. These allusions to the English gothic church, which may have been called for by the rector of the church, are outweighed by the Richardsonian wall, by the blocky massing of the church, and by Kidder's inexplicable use of chateau-style dormers in the tower.

135

Franklin Kidder/Christ Methodist Church, 22nd and Ogden, 1889-91.

Franklin Kidder/Window detail, south facade, Christ Methodist Church, 22nd and Ogden, 1889.

Franklin Kidder/Tower, Asbury Methodist Church, 30th and Vallejo, 1890.

Franklin Kidder/Asbury Methodist Church, 30th and Vallejo, 1890.

Franklin Kidder/Facade detail, Asbury Methodist Church, 30th and Vallejo, 1890.

Kidder's eclecticism was very different from Huddart's. Although he attempted in the Christ Methodist-Episcopal Church to be stylistically flexible and suit his building to the demands or desires of his client, his efforts met with his own resistance. Kidder indulged in eclecticism, but he was basically Richardsonian and admired massive, relatively simple, and well-built buildings. He was not, like Huddart and the Baerresens, an architect of imagery who could mix styles with utter abandon. In the Christ Church, the style of his program was at odds with the basic style of his career. His eclecticism was incomplete and somewhat timid; his basic tendencies as an architect solidly trained in the eastern United States at the height of Richardson's career almost thwarted his attempts to design buildings in different styles.

Franklin Kidder/Asbury Methodist Church, elevation by the architect, 30th and Vallejo, 1890.

An analysis of several Kidder churches will clarify this view of the essential stylistic unity underlying his often eclectic detail. The Saint James Methodist-Episcopal Church built in Denver during 1891 and the larger Asbury Methodist Church erected in 1890 display an extraordinary similarity in massing and plan in spite of the diversity in "style" or effect. The brick and sandstone facade of the Saint James Church possesses a roughly High Victorian character. Its windows are gothic, and the tower gives the whole building a predominant verticality held somewhat in check by horizontal stone banding. The Asbury Church, on the other hand, uses a Richardsonian structural-ornamental system consisting of rounded arches and heavily rusticated stone, yet the plan of both buildings is a compacted version of Richardson's Trinity Church in Boston. Both buildings are chunky and square. They fill their respective lots economically and place all service features in the corner towers. Both buildings are designed "to obtain the greatest capacity, convenience, and architectural expression for the least amount of money."[6]

A careful look at Kidder's published churches reveals a close similarity in basic plans and approaches as well as a diversity in the various styles which he affected. There is little if any consistency in his use of past styles.

Congregational churches are both Richardsonian and High Victorian Gothic, and even the High Victorian varies from church to church— from the relatively loose High Victorian of the First Congregational Church of Longmont with its almost Richardsonian tower to the chunkier and more rectilinear High Victorian of a small congregational church called simply "Design A." In fact, Kidder warned against a straight-jacketed use of styles. He recommended that an "ecclesiastical effect" be given while preserving "as far as possible the architectural conditions."[7]

When compared to the career of Huddart or the Baerresen brothers, Kidder's career appears straightforward and bland. He like Edbrooke applied style or, as he called it, "effect" to his basic building type. He avoided the liberating combinations which are so evident in the buildings of Huddart, and kept the basic differences between buildings to a surface minimum. His writings, such as the monumentally thorough *Architect and Builders Handbook,* stress the practical aspect of architecture and pay little attention to "effects" or styles. He was an architect who was concerned with good, solid, and intelligent architecture, and his temperament was somewhat at odds with the brash and markedly eclectic architecture of the late 1880's and early 1890's.

Franklin Kidder/St. James Methodist Church, 1892– demolished.

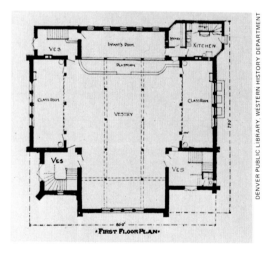

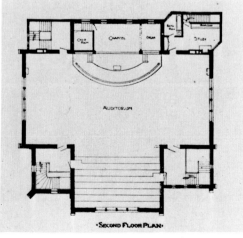

Franklin Kidder/Plan, St. James Methodist Church, Denver, 1892.

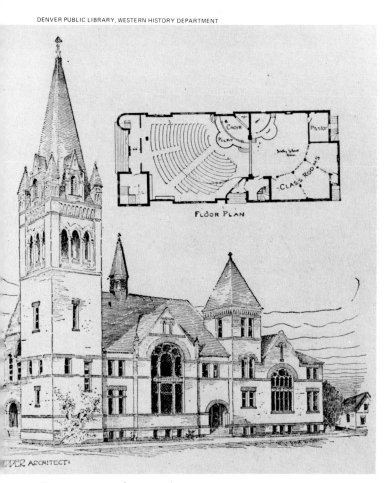

Franklin Kidder/Third Congregational Church, West Denver, elevation by the architect, 1893–demolished.

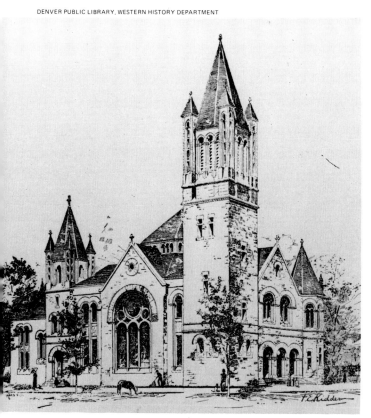

Franklin Kidder/Design C from Churches and Chapels, *1895.*

Franklin Kidder/Design A from Churches and Chapels, *1895.*

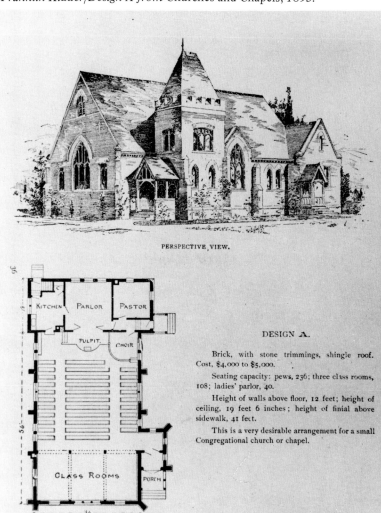

PERSPECTIVE VIEW.

DESIGN A.

Brick, with stone trimmings, shingle roof. Cost, $4,000 to $5,000.

Seating capacity: pews, 236; three class rooms, 108; ladies' parlor, 40.

Height of walls above floor, 12 feet; height of ceiling, 19 feet 6 inches; height of finial above sidewalk, 41 feet.

This is a very desirable arrangement for a small Congregational church or chapel.

FLOOR PLAN.

Franklin Kidder/Design C from Churches and Chapels, *plan, 1895.*

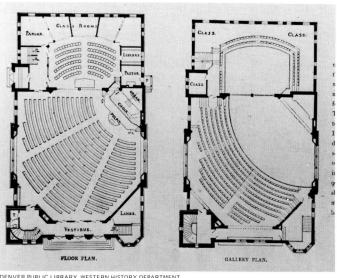

The Baerresen Brothers

The Baerresen brothers, generally known by their initials H.W. and V.E., were, like Huddart, trained in Europe. Their father was a Danish maritime architect, and of his four sons, two became architects and two contractors, and all emigrated to Denver.[8] Their firm was established in 1887 before the inauguration of the great building boom. Their career was moderately successful and they opened an office in Cheyenne in the 1890's. They do not appear to have had an architectural specialty, and their buildings included homes, office buildings, warehouses, a hotel, a church, and innumerable fraternal lodges.

Like their contemporary, J.J. Huddart, the Baerresen brothers seem to have entered a situation in which architectural uniformity was difficult to maintain. Trained in Denmark, they were hardly prepared for the stylistic battle then raging in provincial American architecture. Their initial efforts were reasonably successful imitations of various contemporary American styles. The Flat Building, built in 1890 for Leonard and Montgomery at 20th and California Streets, was predominantly Queen Anne with Stick Style porches and modified Richardsónian details. The Glen Park Cottage, a mountain wayside inn, was one of the purest Shingle Style buildings constructed in Colorado. Its massing showed a knowledge of contemporary architecture in the eastern states and seemed to derive from the tradition of the detached house in Newport. Its closest prototypes are the houses of McKim, Mead, and White in Newport, such as the Isaac Bell residence of 1881-82, and its complex faceted roof and the huge veranda which swooped around the entire house were very unlike the more massive houses being constructed around 1890 in Denver. Another Shingle Style design from around 1890 was a projected mountain hotel for an unspecified site— possibly Manitou Springs. This large building, while more ponderous and heavily roofed than the earlier Wayside Inn, adopted the basic Shingle Style resort paradigm which had been established in the early eighties on the east coast.

Baerresen Brothers/Glen Park Cottage, Wayside Inn, Colorado, 1890.

Baerresen Brothers/Flat Building, terrace for Leonard and Montgomery at 20th and California, 1890–demolished.

Baerresen Brothers/Projected mountain hotel, drawing by the architects, circa 1890.

Baerresen Brothers/The Mack Block, 1890—demolished.

The Shingle Style was totally unsuited to commercial structures, and the Baerresens changed their model to conform to the building type. Their commercial structures are loose and somewhat diffuse versions of the Edbrookian-Chicago style which was fashionable in Denver during the 1880's and 1890's. The Mack Block, their largest building and their office for many years, was a six-story rusticated stone building very like Edbrooke's contemporary Club Building. Its stone detailing, which was unnecessarily shallow, seems to derive from the surface detail of Edbrooke's Essex Building of 1887. In general, the Mack Block was a weakened and almost uncomprehending variation of the very structurally minded Chicago style. Its dependence on early and relatively unsuccessful Edbrooke structures rather than on the more advanced buildings of Chicago or the Edbrooke buildings contemporary with it was unfortunate. The large facade of the building had little of the brittleness and visual strength of an Edbrooke building; the Baerresens were better when they weren't trying to be advanced. Their straightforward and economical warehouse for a Mr. Sheridan on the corner of 17th and Wynkoop is one of the best warehouses built in Denver during the nineteenth century. Sprightly Richardsonian arches on the Wynkoop facade are divided vertically and tension between these vertical pilasters and the arches enlivens the facade considerably. The main 17th Street facade has a generous Palladian surface organization lacking in most other buildings in the area.

Baerresen Brothers/Sheridan Building, 17th and Wynkoop, 1892.

The Baerresens' heavy dependence on Edbrooke's commercial architecture is best seen in a proposed building pictured in their own pamphlet entitled *Booklet of Architectural Views,* published sometime after 1916. This six-story block was probably designed around 1890 and is very close to both Edbrooke's McPhee Block and his slightly earlier Ernest and Cranmer Building. The building is relatively sophisticated in its use of the Edbrookian vocabulary and avoids being a copy, but it lacks the strength of its prototypes and is very timid in its detailing around the front door. The building can be seen as an aesthetic opposite of the buildings of Lang and Pugh or even of Huddart. The Baerresens were architects who used many models for their buildings, but very rarely did they mix their models. When designing a commercial structure, they were almost purely Edbrookian. When designing a terrace, they adopted the same free eclecticism as other architects. However, their general tendency was to simplify their source and make the new building more "tasteful" than its model. They rarely exaggerated their source and consistently avoided compositional tension, preferring symmetry and simplicity to the stylistic "excesses" of Denver's more adventurous architects.

The one almost violently complex building of the Baerresen brothers was, curiously, a church: the Swedish Lutheran Church formerly on the corner of 23rd and Logan Streets. This building was begun in 1890 and

John J. Huddart/Project for the Apex Building, drawing by the architect, 1889.

Baerresen Brothers/Proposed office building, circa 1890.

seems to be related to the basic Kidder church. Kidder may very well have consulted with the Baerresens on the design and construction of this church, as by 1890 he was considered the leading local expert on church architecture. The square building with a corner tower had become almost a paradigm in American church architecture by the end of the century; Saint John's Roman Catholic Church designed in 1880 by Egan and Hill in Chicago is a clear prototype, but there are literally thousands of others, including buildings in Denver. In its use of detail, the Swedish Lutheran Church was more exuberant than any of the Baerresens' other buildings. The enormous gothic arches were aggressively constructed of rusticated sandstone; the tower had enlarged details and a very unecclesiastical castelated corner towerette. Much of the banding and detailing on the shorter of the two front towers may have been derived from Edbrooke's much earlier First Baptist Church. The Swedish Church lacks the consistent and properly proportioned detail which is appropriate to the Kidder church type. It seems related to an earlier and more active aesthetic which, thanks to the retardataire brilliance of William Lang, was very much alive in Denver. When compared to Lang's more exciting Saint Mark's Church, the Swedish Lutheran Church looks rather awkward and even tame. It is one of the only buildings designed by the Baerresens which used an agglomerative eclecticism. They attempted to learn

Baerresen Brothers/Swedish Lutheran Church, 1890–demolished.

145

different lessons from different buildings and this church represented a somewhat bizarre compromise between two conflicting types of architecture, one clear and Richardsonian and the other complex and High Victorian.

Generally, the Baerresen brothers were intelligent eclectics who modeled their buildings after widely accepted types by other, usually local, architects. They did not attempt to forge a new style from a synthetic combination of past architecture. Rather, they replicated buildings as complete objects with varying degrees of success. The Swedish Church was one of their only true aesthetic failures. It was a combination of too many elements, which fought across the facade throughout the history of the building. With this single exception, their buildings depended on single sources—their resort buildings on the Shingle Style, their commercial buildings on Edbrooke and the Chicago school, their homes and terraces on Queen Anne with the addition of some Richardsonian features, and their warehouses on the commercial brick vernacular then universal in the United States.

Baerresen Brothers/Alonzo Thomas residence, 1070 Humboldt, 1895.

PHOTO: EDWARDS AND BROWN

Baerresen Brothers/Interior, Alonzo Thomas residence, 1070 Humboldt, 1895.

Baerresen Brothers/Interior, Alonzo Thomas residence, 1070 Humboldt, 1895.

The Baerresens' greatest eclectic achievement was the marvelously tasteless temple for the El Jebel Shrine on 15th and Sherman in Denver. This building has a predominantly moorish facade with fanciful corner towers and rather Venetian arcades. Exotic detailing is tempered somewhat by prim materials, tightness of detail, and sheer massiveness of the building, yet the triumph of eclecticism is the interior. Instead of mixing styles with the abandon of Lang or Huddart, the Baerresens attempted almost archeological reconstructions of what they imagined to be the great exotic styles of the past and present. Represented are Egyptian, Alhambra, craftsman, Flemish, gothic, Japanese, French Salon, and Empire styles. Each room is separate from the others, and each great style of the past stands in isolated splendor.

Baerresen Brothers/El Jebel Shrine Temple, 1770 Sherman.

Conclusion:

This chapter has been a modest attempt to differentiate between eclectics and to give some reasons for Denver's late eclecticism. Detailed examination of three prominent Denver firms whose careers would be called eclectic by any historian of architecture demonstrates a great deal of difference among the three. All these architects matured in a schizophrenic decade of American architecture in which some architects were trying desperately to clarify architecture and others were involved in an exaggerated flourishing of High Victorian eclecticism. Three of the architects, Kidder and the Baerresen brothers, were caught in the middle of this struggle and did not wholeheartedly adopt either Richardsonianism or late eclecticism. To the Baerresen brothers, Richardsonianism was just another American style with little of the priority which it had for other architects. Kidder, though trained in the Richardsonian mode, could never fully abandon his pursuit of aesthetic "effects." Huddart was the most liberated of the four and probably the most eclectic architect in the city. Unlike Lang, whose buildings exhibited a clear and definable eclectic style, Huddart never came to terms with eclecticism as an architectural theory, and his career is almost unimaginably diverse. His existence and that of the Baerresen brothers in the Denver architectural profession of the late nineteenth century makes secure attributions of many unattributed buildings very difficult. A building may look like a weak Lang or Edbrooke building (and all architects designed at least a few weak buildings) and might easily be by Baerresen or Huddart.

It seems, from a careful analysis of the works of the Baerresens, Huddart, and Kidder, that none of these men particularly cared about the past insofar as it is evoked in eclectic architecture. Rather, they were architects caught somewhat tragically in the middle of a confused battle between the eclectics and the "pure" architects of the eighties. Their architecture undoubtedly displays a use of contemporary architecture as a model rather than a consistent re-evaluation of the past architecture which they alluded to in their buildings. While this observation may also hold true for William Lang, who was by far a greater architect than any of them, the historical thinness of his sources was offset by a prodigious power of formal invention. All these architects built buildings which refer rather generically to "the past," and the modern viewer is not intended to think of twelfth century Venice or of Chartres or of Periclean Athens. Rather, he is intended to imagine a past as seen by a fabulous present which summarizes, violates, and breaks down the achievements of former civilizations by summarizing, violating, and breaking down past architecture.

Architect Unknown/Residence, 929 Pearl. The exuberance of this home suggest William Lang, but the composition is too spare and traditional for Lang. Circa 1889.

149

Richard-sonianism

The Style of the
1880's

HH. Richardson was probably the most influential and important American architect of the later nineteenth century. His career, which began in the mid-1860's with several small High Victorian Gothic churches in Massachusetts, gained prominence only after the construction of Trinity Church in Boston, designed in 1873 and completed in 1877. This building was not the first building in the United States to use Romanesque detailing, but it became the icon for the Romanesque movement in America which was to bear Richardson's name. Its chunkiness, the strength of its masonry construction, and the simplicity of the rounded arch motif used

throughout must have looked both strange and refreshing to a generation raised on the small-scale spikiness of Second Empire and High Victorian buildings. The strength and gravity of Trinity appealed to Americans as did its evocation of a deep and elemental past. Richardson achieved artistic maturity in this building, in spite of the flaws which the detail-oriented nineteenth century critics pointed out in the design. The official organ of national American architecture, the *American Architect and Building News,* criticized the shortness of the nave and the oscillation between conventional and natural detail, but concluded that "for all its faults, however, there is in the work a union of richness and breadth, a singular charm of color, and a noble dignity, that lift it above anything that has been done in the country within our knowledge."[1]

After the dedication of Trinity Church, the *American Architect and Building News* became Richardson's chief supporter until his death in 1886. Photographs of his buildings and drawings of both his architecture and furniture were published with some regularity in the magazine, and, by the middle of the 1880's, "Richardsonian" buildings were known to every American architect.[2] Most American architectural magazines published obituaries at the architect's death in 1886, but it was not until 1888 that Richardsonian literature gained its full strength. In that year, Mariana Griswold Van Rensselaer published her definitive and often brilliant critical biography of Richardson and the *American Architect and Building News* released beautiful photographic booklets of his work in a series entitled *Monographs of American Architecture.* American architecture began to show Richardsonian influences immediately after the publication of the Trinity Church in the *American Architect and Building News.* Only after the group of publications which appeared after Richardson's death did the really national phase of American Richardsonianism begin.

Richardson and the West

Despite the fact that Richardsonian buildings were built all over the country in the late 1880's, many published Richardsonian buildings are from the west or the middle west. There are several reasons for this concentration of Richardsonianism in the provincial regions of the United States. The most obvious reason was Richardson's importance in the history of Chicago architecture. His buildings in Chicago, especially the Marshall Field Warehouse and the McVeagh house, had almost revolutionary importance for the Chicago School in spite of their rather old-fashioned wall-bearing appearance. The effect of Richardson's buildings on the architecture of John Wellborn Root and Louis Sullivan was crucial to the development of younger men into the

H.H. Richardson/Marshall Field Warehouse drawing, 1885-87. Published in Henry Hobson Richardson and His Works.

great architects which they became. Further, Chicago was the archetypal western city. It flourished with renown in the nineties; its spectacular reconstruction after the fire of 1873 made the city an architect's haven. Its development of a monumental commercial architecture in the middle of the 1880's was well known to all major American cities, and its fabled "skyscrapers" provided prototypes for American, and especially western, commercial architecture for generations.

Perhaps more important than this immediate competitive connection between the burgeoning western cities was the fact that Richardsonian architecture was chosen as the foremost style of this competition. Westerners had always been very conscious of the grandness and largeness of "their" land. Landscape painting of the mid-century had given the west an image of heroic scale and awesome magnificence in the minds of the miners, the opportunists, and the health-seekers. Photographs by the greatest and most famous photographer of the west, W.H. Jackson, popularized the impression of vast scale and endless expanse by adopting the same compositional techniques as the great painter, Bierstadt. Jackson photographed valleys from the highest possible point; he hung from cliffs and balanced precariously on

pinnacles; he photographed rocky regions with an eye for scale and ruthlessness. Westerners wanted buildings in keeping with the monumental splendor of their land, and they consciously sought a strong and vital architecture. Nowhere is their sentiment better or more succinctly expressed than in an article entitled "The City House in the West," which appeared in the October 1890 issue of *Scribner's Magazine*.

"In Denver we have on the one side the broad expanse of the plains, and on the other the high mountains. No architect is qualified for the best class of work in Denver who does not take these two great facts into consideration. Denver architecture should be characterized by strength, solidity, and richness."
How similar the last words sound to the *American Architect and Building News* in describing Trinity Church in 1877 in terms of "richness," "breadth," and "a noble dignity." In fact, many Denver architects seem to have considered Richardsonian Romanesque to be an almost exclusively institutional style. The heavy imagery— stone, weightbearing walls, generous rounded arches, rusticated banding in the stone— all suggested institutional grandeur rather than small-scale domesticity.

151

Denver's connection with the heavy and grounded architecture of Richardson was furthered by its most prominent architects. Frank E. Edbrooke maintained close family connections with Chicago throughout the eighties. Franklin Kidder came to Denver in 1888 from Richardson's city, Boston, and his career showed a consistent and often remarkable knowledge of the master's architecture. Another frequent connection with Richardsonianism was the Boston firm of Andrews, Jacques, and Rantoul, which maintained a Denver office.

Architect Unknown/Richardsonian window from the main facade of the house at 131 Sherman, circa 1889.

Frank E. Edbrooke/Rusticated stone wall, carriage house, Warren residence, 2160 South Cook, 1892.

Miller and Janisch/Stone detail, South Broadway Christian Church, 23 Lincoln, 1890.

Robert Roeschlaub/Rusticated stone wall, University Hall, Denver University, 1890.

Varian and Sterner (?)/Richardsonian window detail, residence, 900 Logan, circa 1889.

Denver's Richardsonianism

Richardsonianism operated in Denver as the counter-offensive to the late High Victorian eclectic architecture practiced in the city until 1893. Its massive walls and round arches were very attractive to Denverites and their architects. The strength and importance of Edbrooke, a confirmed Richardsonian, and the fact that many of the city's later prominent architects began their Denver careers as draftsmen in Edbrooke's office, explains the Richardsonian complexion of Denver's building boom.[3]

Richardson's influence on Denver architecture was extraordinarily diverse. Buildings as different as Huddart's Kinneavy Terrace and Jackson's Treate Hall for Colorado Women's College, both completed in 1889, share Richardsonian features which are undeniable. Yet with the exception of a few clear and relatively isolated examples, the character of Denver's Richardsonianism is difficult to break down and analyze. Huddart's Lipe Terrace and Lang's Everts house exhibit features derived from the so-called Romanesque revival as popularized by Richardson, but these features, most significantly the rounded arch, are not unique to Richardson and are only one of many possible "styles" used in combination by eclectics such as Huddart and Lang. Although Lang's Everts house displayed a possible connection with the Ames Gate Lodge, one of Richardson's most popular buildings, it need not have derived the round hipped dormers from Richardson directly. Lang and Huddart, in most of their architecture, seem to be Richardsonians at least once removed from the "source" in Richardson's own career.

John J. Huddart/Kinneavy Terrace, 27th and Stout, 1889.

John J. Huddart/Lipe Terrace

154

William Lang/Everts house, 1889-90—demolished.

H.H. Richardson/F.L. Ames Gate Lodge, North Easton, Mass., 1880-81. Published in The Architecture of H.H. Richardson and His Times.

Source Problems

The word "source" must be used with some caution in discussing art or architecture in the latter nineteenth century, especially architecture in the 1880's. As noted previously, Denver architects subscribed to most of the architectural national and regional magazines published in the United States. These magazines were often extremely well illustrated and did not favor "famous" architects in their choice of buildings to illustrate. In spite of his national fame and the consistently high quality of his work, Richardson's own work was not published extensively, but illustrations of a great many buildings which probably derived from his work appeared often. Consequently a confusion between Richardson and Richardsonianism would have been common and even understandable among many architects unaware of the actual architectural milieu in Boston. In fact, a great many western Richardsonian architects learned "Richardsonianism" not from Richardson himself, but from other Richardsonians. By the late eighties the beautiful and wildly Romantic architecture of Leroy Buffington, the most prominent architect in Minneapolis, was perhaps the most widely published "Richardsonian" architecture in the United States, in spite of the vast differences between his imagistic work and Richardson's solid and brooding architecture. It is probable that Buffington, Root of Chicago and the innumerable minor architects whose work was published in the national press, provided the provincial city of Denver with its Richardsonian models. It is thus not always possible to point out a single source for a provincial building in Richardson's career. Not only do the published Richardsonian buildings complicate any clear theory of influence, but Richardson's own use, re-use, and, occasionally, mis-use of his architectural techniques add to the confusion. His famous library type with its central gable, side tower, and entrance arch was probably derived from church architecture and was used in his Ames Gate Lodge as well as the libraries in their various versions.

Richardsonian window, circa 1889.

Varian and Sterner/Rusticated stone wall, Denver Athletic Club, 1325 Glenarm Place, 1889-90.

H. H. Richardson/F. L. Ames Gate Lodge, north side, North Easton, Mass., 1880-81. Published in The Architecture of H. H. Richardson and His Times.

H. H. Richardson/Crane Memorial Library, Quincy, Mass., 1880. Published in Henry Hobson Richardson and His Works.

The Library Type

The more popular of Richardson's types among Denver architects of the nineteenth century were those of the library, mentioned above, the Allegheny Courthouse, and the closely related Albany City Hall. One Denver transformation of the library type is even more interesting and strange to the modern eye: the Fairmount Cemetery entrance gate, designed by Harry Wendell. The gate is a gothic version of a Richardson library. While no one library is the obvious and single source, the Billings Library completed shortly after Richardson's death in 1886 is perhaps the closest prototype. The transformation into gothic is, surprisingly enough, very successful in spite of the stylistic impurities. The pointed arches, the detached gable, and the columnettes at entrance give the building more levity and grace than the Richardson prototype, and the Fairmount entrance gate is, perhaps, the most original and beautiful Richardsonian building in Denver.

Denver's most subliminal example of the library type is the Iliff School of Theology at the University of Denver. Built in 1892, the building was probably designed by Edbrooke, who was the architect of the Warren-Illiff family. Its program is roughly similar to Richardson's Sever Hall at Harvard, one of the least imitated of Richardson's masterpieces. Instead of designing a building based on Sever Hall, Edbrooke or one of his designers chose a modified library plan which was increased in scale to fit the program. The arcade above the entrance arch and the polygonal wing both recall the various schemes for the Billings Library, although Edbrooke's building suffers in comparison to its prototype. Again gothic detail is applied to a roughly Richardsonian building with a reasonable degree of success. Chateauesque dormers help counteract the predominant horizontality of the facade, and derive possibly from the Cincinatti Chamber of Commerce project, the Allegheny Courthouse, or, perhaps, the Gratwick House in Buffalo.

Harry T.E. Wendell/Entrance gate, Fairmount Cemetery, 1889-90.

H. H. Richardson/Billings Library, Burlington, Vermont, 1883-86. Published in The Architecture of H. H. Richardson and His Times.

Frank E. Edbrooke (?)/East facade, Iliff School of Theology, 1892.

Frank E. Edbrooke (?)/Iliff School of Theology, 1892.

H.H. Richardson/Sever Hall, Cambridge, Mass., 1878-80. Published in Henry Hobson Richardson and His Works.

Frank E. Edbrooke (?)/Detail, main facade, Iliff School of Theology, 1892.

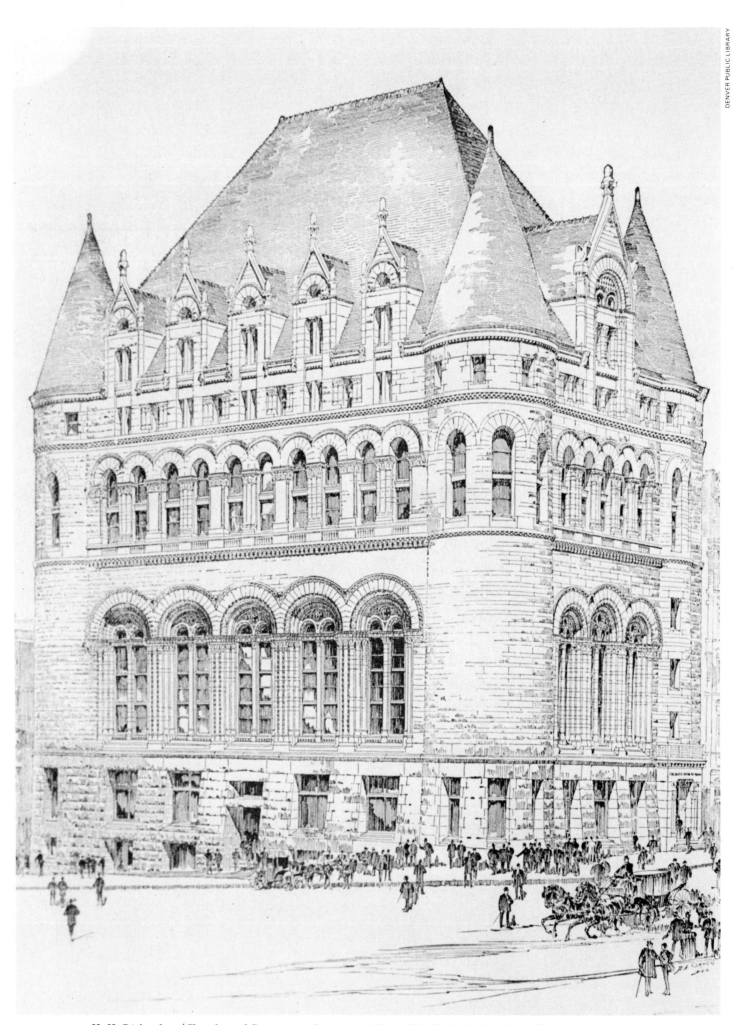

H. H. Richardson/Chamber of Commerce, Cincinnati, Ohio, 1885. Published in Henry Hobson Richardson and His Works.

162

H. H. Richardson/Allegheny County buildings, Pittsburgh, Pennsylvania, 1884. Published in Henry Hobson Richardson and His Works.

H. H. Richardson/City Hall, Albany, New York, 1880. Published in Henry Hobson Richardson and His Works.

The City Hall Type

Richardson's library type proved the most versatile and often reproduced massing type from his career. His larger public buildings, in spite of their quality and popularity, were more difficult to replicate in miniature and were thought suited only to very large institutional buildings. Edbrooke and Kidder built buildings on the model of the larger Richardson buildings; the Central Presbyterian Church and the Asbury Methodist Church were both derived from the Albany City Hall, in spite of their differences in scale and their handling of proportion. Kidder's Asbury Church was probably the more Richardsonian of the two in its enlargement of details and its sophisticated polychromy. The Central Church is much sparer, simpler, and more coloristically unified. The walls are sheer and relatively unadorned; they rise with a thin and expansive grace quite unlike the stone upon stone horizontality of Asbury Church or of the Richardson prototype in Albany. The thinness and stretched quality of the Edbrooke building is almost exaggerated in the tower. Whereas Richardson made his elongated corner tower almost solid stone, Edbrooke cut his away into long, thin lantern openings topped by ogee arches. This tendency to elongate, to accent vertical elements, to avoid the groundedness of Richardson is characteristic of Edbrooke's Richardsonian architecture. The Loretto Heights building, derived from Richardson's Allegheny Courthouse, has none of the chunkiness and solidity of the parent building. Edbrooke strained for height, lightness, and delicacy, none of which are particularly Richardsonian qualities. Edbrooke used Richardsonian architecture less consistently than Kidder, whose Asbury Methodist Church is Denver's only really closely Richardsonian building.

Frank E. Edbrooke/Central Presbyterian Church, 1660 Sherman, 1890-92.

165

Frank E. Edbrooke/College of Loretto, 1890-91.

H. H. Richardson/Trinity Church, Boston, Massachusetts, 1879. Published in Henry Hobson Richardson and His Works.

Franklin Kidder/Asbury Methodist Church, 30th and Vellejo, 1890.

L. DEV. REGNIER, PHOT.

The Asbury Church, at the corner of 30th and Vallejo, derives its massing from Richardson's Albany City Hall. This connection is not total, owing to the functional differences between the two buildings and to Kidder's basic eclecticism as a Richardsonian architect. Sited prominently on a hillside in the Highlands, the church has engaged in a great dialogue of the Richardsonian towers since 1890. The towers of Asbury, Loretto Heights and Central Presbyterian Church, all deriving from the square tower of the Allegheny and the Albany buildings, converse above the hustle of downtown and give the city a great deal of its Richardsonian character. The Asbury Church derives its facade detail in large part from the Trinity Church in Boston and its progeny throughout the United States. The polychrome stone bands are intended to hold the wall together visually and to fill up what would have been an excessively large and rather blank stone facade. In most of his Richardsonian architecture, Kidder shared with Richardson the desire to fill up, to complete, to enlarge architectural detail, to lavish attention on every part of the building. Edbrooke, on the other hand, did not possess this inclination and designed blander and, in many cases, more systematic Richardsonian architecture than Kidder. Kidder's Richardsonianism often follows the master's tendency toward massively walled and rather heavy architecture rather than precisely replicating Richardson buildings. The Asbury Methodist Church was perhaps the only building in Kidder's career which is identifiably close to a Richardson prototype.

Franklin Kidder/Door detail, Asbury Methodist Church, 30th and Vallejo, 1890.

Franklin Kidder/Stone detail, tower, Asbury Methodist Church, 30th and Vallejo, 1890.

Franklin Kidder/Tower, Asbury Methodist Church, 30th and Vallejo, 1890.

Franklin Kidder/Staircase tower, Asbury Methodist Church, 30th and Vallejo, 1890.

Richardsonian Elements:
The Massive Wall and Round Arch

Rather than imitating Richardson's building types, most Denver architects chose instead to borrow the rusticated stone walls and huge round arches which dominated the master's career. These architectural motifs were used in a variety of contexts. Many buildings which exhibited stylistic features from the Shingle Style or the Renaissance revival also utilized these characteristically Richardsonian features. Such buildings as the North Denver Church, Treate Hall, and the South Broadway Christian Church reflect this type of influence from Richardson's career.

Franklin Kidder/Detail, North Denver Church, 933 East 24th Avenue, 1890.

Franklin Kidder/Entrance detail, North Denver Church 933 East 24th Avenue, 1890.

The North Denver Church

Kidder's North Denver Church at the corner of 24th and Ogden Streets, was even blockier, squatter, and heavier than his Asbury Church. Designed in 1890 and constructed at a cost of around $50,000, the church and tower are a less expensive version of the Asbury Church. The Sunday School and church offices were placed to the side of the building rather than tucked below the sanctuary, and this spreading of the building laterally gives the church an independence from any precise Richardsonian source. The "lava" stone, as it was called in the nineteenth century, is monochromatic, heavily rusticated, and laid in horizontal bands— a technique which Richardson used in his later large buildings. Indeed, the huge size of the stones and their repetitive design is definitely late Richardson in character. The building's Richardsonianism lies in its massive walls and its round arches.

Franklin Kidder/North Denver Church, 933 East 24th Avenue, 1890.

Franklin Kidder/North Denver Church, 933 East 24th Avenue, 1890.

173

*Preliminary Sketch for Chamberlin Observatory. Courtesy:
Special Collections, Denver University Library.*

Chamberlin Observatory

Chamberlin Observatory, begun in 1889 for the University of Denver, is decidedly more Richardsonian than University Hall in spite of its timid lateral wings and the "false-front" separation of the stone entrance arch from the rest of the building. An observatory was not a program encountered frequently by the nineteenth century architect, and it is not surprising that Roeschlaub seems to have chosen a prototype which had been recently published in the *American Architect and Building News* – the observatory built in 1887 for Carleton College in Northfield, Minnesota.

Robert Roeschlaub/Tie rod anchor, Chamberlin Observatory, 2900 East Warren, 1889.

Robert Roeschlaub/Chamberlin Observatory, 2900 East Warren, 1889.

Robert Roeschlaub/East facade, Chamberlin Observatory, 2900 East Warren, 1889.

Treate Hall

Another Richardsonian university building worthy of some discussion was Treate Hall, the first building for Colorado Women's College. Designed early in 1889 by Jackson and Betts, a firm which oddly built no other important buildings in the city, its stonework is surprisingly similar to that of the Denver Club, built in the same year. The lumpiness of the massing, the enlarged details, and the attention paid to "structural" aspects of the facade are all early Richardson in their inspiration. Treate Hall has more to do with the Richardson of Trinity Church and the Ames Building than it does with the more ruthless and sober Richardson of 1885-86. The massing of Treate Hall is relatively monolithic, and the architect enlivened the silhouette with an entrance pavillon, protruding gables, and chateau-style dormers. The asymmetry of the library type is maintained, but there are few allusions to any specific building in Richardson's career. The grand entrance arch is juxtaposed against a very un-Richardsonian bay window. Treate Hall, like Kidder's North Denver Church, is a Richardsonian building with very little direct connection to any building in Richardson's career. Jackson emphasized the structural character of Richardson's buildings— the preponderance of the wall, the round arched window, and horizontal banding.

H.H. Richardson/Ames Building, Boston, Mass., 1882-83.
Published in Henry Hobson Richardson and His Works.

F. H. Jackson/Treate Hall, Colorado Women's College, 1889.

South Broadway Christian Church

The South Broadway Christian Church has many stylistic features which are not Richardsonian. However, its use of Queen Anne gables and a High Victorian massing system is countered by Romanesque arches, very heavily rusticated walls, and an unusual simplicity of wall treatment. In these ways, the South Broadway Christian Church evidences the architects' familiarity with the later architecture of H.H. Richardson.

Miller and Janisch/Carving detail, South Broadway Christian Church, 23 Lincoln, 1890.

Miller and Janisch/Gable detail, South Broadway Christian Church, 23 Lincoln, 1890.

Miller and Janisch/Tower, South Broadway Christian Church, 23 Lincoln, 1890.

Miller and Janisch/Detail, South Broadway Christian Church, 23 Lincoln, 1890.

Miller and Janisch/Entrance detail, South Broadway Christian Church, 23 Lincoln, 1890.

Decorative Richardsonianism:
The Mining Exchange Building

With the exception of the buildings already mentioned and the institutional architecture of Varian and Sterner, a great deal of Denver's institutional and commercial architecture was only weakly influenced by Richardson himself. Most Denver architects simply applied the decorative motifs of Richardsonian architecture to buildings which have little else Richardsonian about them. Examples of this decoration are almost endless and of varying quality. The most famous, even extravagant Richardsonian building of this type was the old Mining Exchange Building designed by the St. Louis firm of Kirchner and Kirchner, which had an office in Denver. The building is almost a catalogue of Richardsonian "features" placed in an almost totally un-Richardsonian context; the rusticated stone arch, the rather stumpy columns, the exaggerated classical moldings, the neo-Romanesque capitals and the horizontal or vertical groupings of windows formed continuous compositions. The building had an exuberance which seemed to hark back to the then "old-fashioned" Denver of the 1870's and early 1880's. The central tower, which Edbrooke tried so hard to suppress, was celebrated in the Mining Exchange Building. The details were thick in their roundness and fullness. The symbolism was rich, associative, and almost incoherently complex. The great monsters, the lion and the bear, snarled at each other across the yawning entrance arch, and the huge, almost heroic miner stared out to the expanse of the great plains stretching north in front of the mountains.

This kind of exuberance is not normally associated with Richardson's architecture, but it was a large component of Richardsonian architecture in the west. Any sustained look at the architecture of Minneapolis, Chicago and Denver in the decade between 1885 and 1895 will reveal a radically active and exciting kind of

Richardsonian architecture which must be seen in strict contrast to the kind of Richardsonianism characterized by strength, solidity, and richness. This new Richardsonianism, which was noticed and criticized by Montgomery Schuyler in 1890, was more decidedly High Victorian in its complexity, its juxtaposition of forms, its active silhouettes, and its picturesque surface activity. The Mining Exchange Building was the most visible and the largest of the buildings in this mode built in Denver. William Lang's houses were better buildings than the Kirchners' Mining Exchange, but they were less visible and noticeably more eclectic.

The Mining Exchange Building provided the model for at least one smaller building in Denver. The Sherman School seems to be a milder version of the Mining Exchange Building with more institutional sobriety. It can be seen in contrast to the other schools of the early 1890's. The stern and safe look of respectable architecture began to take over the city in the 1890's as the century drew to a close. Schools like the Webster School are examples of this safer Richardsonianism. Webster had a closed and secure objectness; it was monochromatic and lacking in the forceful tower and rather humorous ornament which is so evident in the Sherman School. Indeed, the vocabulary of Richardson proved enormously diverse for the Denver architect. Whether used alone or in combination with other styles, Richardsonianism prevailed in that terribly intense and creative decade before the crash. The sober and righteous aspects of Richardsonianism— the style of substantial institutions— countered the more literary use of Romanesque as a style of the past which the architect could combine with other styles to form a new and active whole. The Richardsonianism of the Denver Club must be seen in opposition to the Richardsonianism of the Mining Exchange Building, the Sherman School, or the South Broadway Christian Church.

Kirchner & Kirchner/Mining Exchange Building, circa 1891 – demolished.

Domestic Richardsonianism

The general observation can be made that domestic Richardsonianism is more eclectic and less derived from specific Richardson sources than the institutional architecture. Richardsonian architecture was very appropriate to the castelated mode which was a minor current in Denver domestic architecture after the construction of the notorious Richthofen castle in 1883. Huddart's castle for the Kittredge family was built in competition with Baron Richthofen's castle and shows a decided Richardsonian character. Other examples of Richardsonianism in domestic architecture relate more closely to the master's early career which could be best described as Queen Anne eclectic. A house like Cutshaw's Woodbury residence of 1890 is remarkably similar to Richardson's famous Watts Sherman house in its massing even though the details are more eclectic and for the time old-fashioned than Richardson's were in 1876. The Woodbury residence is an archetypally western version of the Richardsonian Queen Anne Watts Sherman house. The details are enlarged and activated. Most of the forms are in violent or at least uncomfortable juxtaposition. The aborted tower is shoved into the corner, the recessed paneled gable in the main facade almost touches the side of the dominant gable, few forms are complete and the general Langian character of the house is much more apparent than its almost subliminal Richardsonianism. A house on the corner of 14th and Josephine which still stands unattributed is

John J. Huddart/Second Kittredge house (Montclair), 1893–demolished.

Richthofen Castle, 7012 East 12th Avenue

182

one of two or three houses in Denver which used Richardson's aggressively over-scaled stonework. This house, which must be by William Lang, places enormous Richardsonian arches in a context of the late Queen Anne gabled street house. Again, the combinative aesthetic is anything but Richardsonian, but only the Richardson of the Allegheny County prison building could be the prototype for the fabulously over-structured lower story of this house.

The increasing simplification of the house into a single volume has already been discussed. Richardson was one of the principals in this tendency toward simplified architecture, but many of the houses exhibiting this objectness were by other architects. The modern viewer is hard-pressed to find a house in Denver which derives from the Glessner house or the McVeagh house, to name only the more important of Richardson's simple houses in Chicago. These houses probably had more effect in Chicago than they did in more distant Denver or Minneapolis. Only Edbrooke seems to have responded systematically to the Richardsonian challenge, and even his houses do not appear to derive directly from Richardson's own domestic architecture.

H. H. Richardson/Sherman house, Newport, Rhode Island, 1874. Published in The Architecture of H.H. Richardson and His Times.

I. Cutshaw/The Roger Woodbury house, 1889—demolished.

William Lang(?)/Porch detail, residence, 14th and Josephine, circa 1892.

William Lang(?)/Residence, 14th and Josephine, circa 1892.

H. H. Richardson/Franklin McVeagh house, Chicago, Illinois 1885. Published in Henry Hobson Richardson and His Works.

H. H. Richardson/Glessner house, Chicago, Illinois, 1885-87. Published in The Architecture of H. H. Richardson and His Times.

Varian and Sterner

Perhaps Denver's most notable Richardsonian architects were Varian and Sterner, who worked as a partnership in Denver beginning in 1885. Little information about them survives, but the several buildings which can be securely attributed to them are of a high quality rare in Denver Richardsonianism.[4]

The Denver Club

The Denver Club was the most important of the early Colorado clubs and continues to be a haven for influential men today. The original building, at the corner of 17th and Glenarm, was completed in 1889, and the architects designed everything in the building as well as the physical structure itself. The inspiration was distinctly Richardsonian even down to the furniture, which derived from Richardson's furniture published in both the *American Architect and Building News* and Van Rensselaer's biography. The building was one of the

H. H. Richardson/Chair, Converse Memorial Public Library, Malden, Massachusetts, 1883. Published in Henry Hobson Richardson and His Works.

Varian and Sterner/The Denver Club, 1889—demolished.

first totally architect-designed buildings constructed in Denver. Its furniture was made in the city and the architects supervised all the decoration. This must be seen in marked contrast to the earlier important buildings of the city and even to the houses for Denver's wealthy built in the late eighties. These latter buildings contained as many "imports" as possible— the wall paper, the furniture, the dishes, the stained glass, even the often standardized woodwork. In fact, most Denver buildings were conglomerates of divergent and exotic fixtures even into the eighties and early nineties. The fact that a young but influential group of men who commissioned the Denver Club building were interested in a local work of art is indicative of a profound change in Denver's culture and a change which recognized the artistic excellence of local architects and local crafts-men. Varian and Sterner rose to the occasion by designing a highly satisfactory and even rather good Richardsonian building. The Richardsonian style of the Denver Club must be seen as an important proof that Richardsonianism was considered the predominant style of the west by 1889. Its presence as the total style of a building which was built to celebrate local talent for a local-regional group of prominent men can lead the modern viewer to few other conclusions.

In terms of the types of Richardsonianism discussed above, the Denver Club was most closely related to the Richardsonianism of Kidder and Jackson. The massing of the building did not seem to be derived from Richardson's career in any important sense. The details, the stonework, the massiveness, and the solidity of the building were all decidedly Richardsonian. The poly-chromed stone work— dark on the first level and structural trim for the remainder of the building— seems to relate quite closely to the stonework of Richardson's early buildings like the oft-mentioned Trinity Church. The surface was denser and fussier than a Richardson surface; rounded arches crowded each other on the facade, finicky dormers formed a dense cluster, and a massive entrance arch expanded outward to form one of the grandest entrance spaces in Denver. Varian and Sterner were not content with building a moderately Richardsonian building. They clearly wanted the most Richardsonian structure in the world. Almost all the elements of Richardson's style were present, crammed into the relatively small surface with a great deal of sensitivity.

The success of the Denver Club was phenomenal. The *Western Architect and Building News* featured it pro-minently in several issues early in publication. The furniture was reproduced frequently and became the model for a great deal of regional Richardsonian furniture. The building was a singular example of the dark richness of the eighties which stood solidly and safely until destroyed by the wrecker's ball in 1952.

The Denver Athletic Club

Varian and Sterner received the commission for another prestigious Denver club, the Denver Athletic Club, between 14th and 15th Streets on Glenarm. This building is noticeably different the Denver Club. Its basic form is a commercial street front building, and its facade is Richardsonian with a Denver accent. The first two levels are rusticated stone cut in monumental blocks reminiscent of the Allegheny Prison in Pittsburgh. The upper levels are constructed of local brick laid in Richardsonian arches. The building has an almost implacable flatness. The levels are distinct from one another and there is very little surface relief like that found in Edbrooke's buildings of 1888 and 1889. The cornice is markedly classical, but it is decidedly more delicate than any of Richardson's classical cornices and relates more closely to the Edbrooke of the McPhee Block and the Brown Hotel. The building survives in a remarkable state of preservation today. It forms a monument to Denver's own Richardsonianism; the fusion of Edbrookian and Richardsonian is complete. The local style of the upper floors acknowledges its debt to the national style of the lower floors.

Varian and Sterner/First floor detail, Denver Athletic Club, 1325 Glenarm Place, 1889-90.

Varian and Sterner/Carving at the entrance arch, Denver Athletic Club, 1325 Glenarm Place, 1889-90.

Varian and Sterner/Brick Richardsonian arches, Denver Athletic Club, 1325 Glenarm Place, 1889-90.

Varian and Sterner/Grill detail, Denver Athletic Club, 1325 Glenarm Place, 1889-90.

Varian and Sterner/First floor detail, Denver Athletic Club, 1325 Glenarm Place, 1889-90.

Varian and Sterner/The Denver Athletic Club, 1325 Glenarm, 1889-90.

H.H. Richardson/Allegheny County Jail, Pittsburgh, Pennsylvania 15101. 1884-86. Published in The Architecture of H.H. Richardson and His Times.

Frank E. Edbrooke/The H.C. Brown Hotel, 321 17th Street, 1890-92.

Frank E. Edbrooke/McPhee Block, circa 1889.

The Holzman House and Charlene Place

The two other Varian and Sterner buildings worthy of note in this context are the Solomon Holzman house, formerly at 1772 Grant Street, and the Charlene terrace at 1421-1441 Pennsylvania Street. Both buildings are examples of the so-called chateau style which was so popular in Denver in the later 1880's and early 1890's. Both buildings were constructed in 1890 and are obviously closely related to one another. Their Richardsonianism is marked; they can be compared to the later Richardson houses, most notably the Gratwick house in Buffalo, and to the Richardson of the Cincinnati Chamber of Commerce. Chateau features such as the frontally flattened dormers and the accent on vertical elements such as gables and turrets were adopted by Richardson in the later years of his career and were exaggerated in the provincial architecture of Leroy

Buffington. Chateau-style buildings were constructed in Denver throughout the later eighties; prominent examples include the Boethel residence, formerly on Colfax Avenue, and the existing Croke mansion at the corner of 11th Avenue and Pennsylvania. Varian and Sterner simplified the chateau style as it was exemplified in the Boethel and Croke mansions and made it markedly more Richardsonian. The walls were massive stone and the arches were almost overstructured. The porches were solid and even a bit foreboding in their resoluteness. The terrace, which was built for Charles H. Smith at a cost of $75,000, consists of a large house for the Smiths with three terraced houses adjacent. As it stands today, its sandstone facade is considerably weathered and its porch plastered and glassed so that the building is almost unrecognizable.

Varian and Sterner/Holzman house, 1890–demolished.

Varian and Sterner/Charlene Place Apartments, 1421-1441 Pennsylvania, 1890.

H. H. Richardson/Gratwick house, Buffalo, New York, 1886-89. Published in The Architecture of H. H. Richardson and His Times.

Conclusion

Richardsonianism has proved an extraordinarily diverse phenomenon. Some architects, like Edbrooke and Wendell, chose to emulate Richardson's building types, often with changes in style and detail. Other architects, like Kidder, Jackson, and occasionally Varian and Sterner, chose to adapt the Richardsonian structural tendencies and imagery to their own ends. The rusticated stone and the rounded arch were the hallmark of Richardsonianism in Denver, and their existence in buildings which are not even vaguely Richardsonian in other ways indicates the importance of the style to High Victorian architects in America. William Lang, J.J. Huddart, and the other Denver eclectics used Richardsonianism along with all the other fashionable styles and, in so doing, expressed their often willful misunderstanding of the movement. Richardsonianism represented a new style to America in the middle 1880's and into the 1890's. Its simplicity and its structural (as opposed to additive ornamental) vocabulary were seen as a hard and rational counter to the confusion of the eclectic movement in America. Richardsonian buildings were *basic* buildings to western Americans, buildings which they described as grand, solid, broad, rich, dignified, and strong. The great rusticated arches unified and structured buildings; they spoke of an ambiguous and marvelous past, a past both Roman and Romanesque. The rusticated stone walls were strong, safe, and secure, and they stood as a marvelous counter to the Rocky Mountains, organizing the emptiness of the great plains.

PHOTO: EDWARDS AND BROWN

William Lang(?)/Residence, 1407 Humboldt. This house displayed the influence of Richardsonianism in its overscaled and almost violently rusticated stone. Its massing derives ultimately from the Queen Anne house, and its details are severely neo-Renaissance. Circa 1892.

William Lang (?)/Residence, 12th and Pennsylvania, 1889-90.

Frank E. Edbrooke/Residence, 12th and Pennsylvania, circa 1890.

Architect Unknown/D. Fletcher residence. One of many Richardsonian stone houses built in Denver in the early nineties. The sobriety, the bulkiness, and the insistent rectilinear quality of the Fletcher house looked forward to Denver's post-crash architecture. Circa 1891–demolished.

William Lang (?)/Porch detail, residence, 14th and Josephine, circa 1892.

H. H. Richardson/Entrance, Ames Memorial Public Library, North Easton, Massachusetts, 1877. Published in Henry Hobson Richardson *and His Works.*

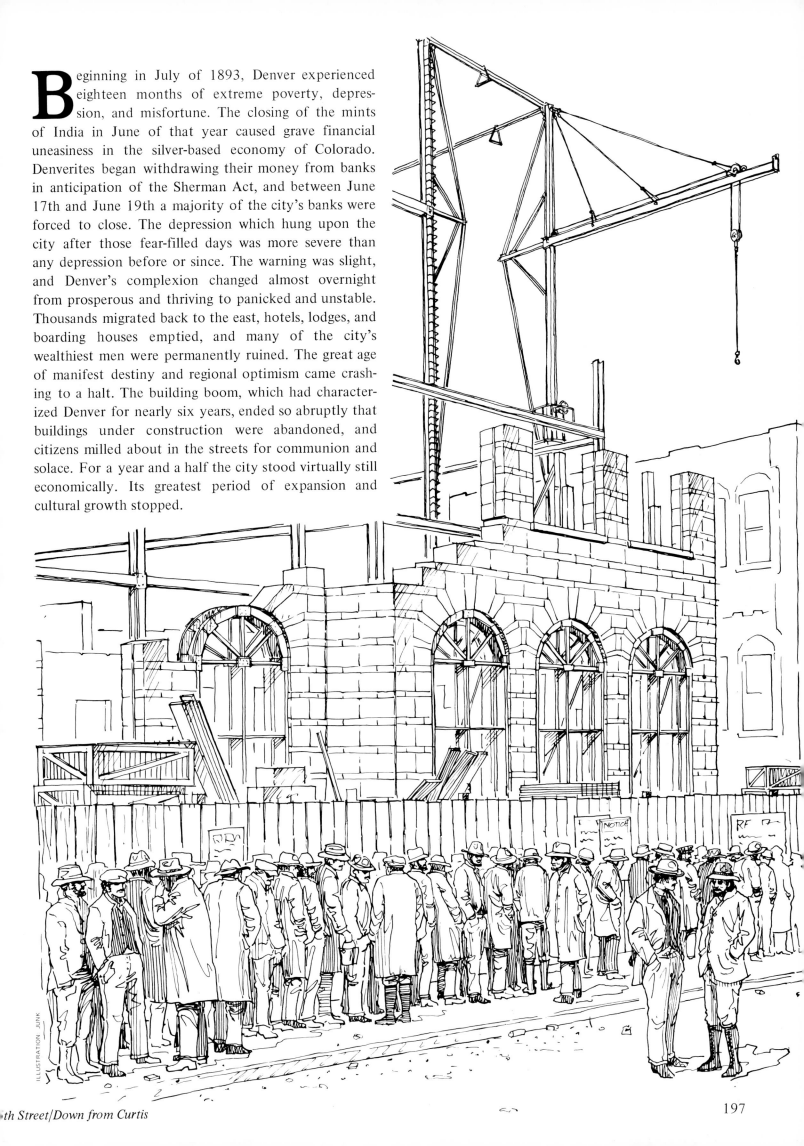

Beginning in July of 1893, Denver experienced eighteen months of extreme poverty, depression, and misfortune. The closing of the mints of India in June of that year caused grave financial uneasiness in the silver-based economy of Colorado. Denverites began withdrawing their money from banks in anticipation of the Sherman Act, and between June 17th and June 19th a majority of the city's banks were forced to close. The depression which hung upon the city after those fear-filled days was more severe than any depression before or since. The warning was slight, and Denver's complexion changed almost overnight from prosperous and thriving to panicked and unstable. Thousands migrated back to the east, hotels, lodges, and boarding houses emptied, and many of the city's wealthiest men were permanently ruined. The great age of manifest destiny and regional optimism came crashing to a halt. The building boom, which had characterized Denver for nearly six years, ended so abruptly that buildings under construction were abandoned, and citizens milled about in the streets for communion and solace. For a year and a half the city stood virtually still economically. Its greatest period of expansion and cultural growth stopped.

ILLUSTRATION JUNK

th Street/Down from Curtis

In many ways, the nineteenth century ended for Denver in 1893. This great century of expansion, invention, and experimentation lay exhausted and ruined for Denverites, and its attitude, its population, and its architecture changed dramatically after 1893. The pinwheel plan, projecting gables, sky-piercing chimneys, mixtures of intentionally disparate styles, and ruggedly rusticated stone walls almost disappeared from Denver architecture. Edbrooke's sober, post-Richardson architecture in the eighties had set the stage for a new Denver of rather boxy, unornamented, and restrained buildings. Architects like Marshall Pugh and William Lang left the city, and men like J.J. Huddart tamed their architecture to fit the new aesthetic confines of a changed city. Huddart's later houses as well as those of the Baerresen brothers were simple brick boxes with hipped roofs, few projecting dormers, symmetrical handling of features, and very little "style," as it would have been defined by the eclectics of the 1880's. The era of great commercial architecture was over, and Edbrooke's later buildings were plain, inelegant, and decidedly unimportant architectural achievements. Denver submerged for a decade or so, and, when construction rose and the population stabilized at the end of the century, efforts were concentrated on "filling up" the city which had been so greatly expanded in the building boom.

The Campion residence

1718 Gaylord

1110 Humbolt

1740 Gaylord

Denver architecture of the later 1890's is curiously comparable to its architecture of the 1870's. The buildings were plain, generally symmetrical, and boxy. Great attention was paid to the roof and its bracketed over-hang, and decoration was applied with economy and considered appropriate only to certain areas within the building. Tour de force efforts of carving, stained glass, brick-work, and room arrangements were infrequent in the later 1890's. Building was regularized again, and houses appeared in almost monotonous rows as if they had been lifted from the same pattern book. Of course, a few very wealthy families survived the period of the crash unscathed and continued to construct lavish mansions throughout the later nineties. Yet even these mansions showed evidence of the profound change which occurred within Denver society. They were generally classical, rather pompous, and plain. Their rooms were displaced with a greater symmetry around central halls, and they were set back further from the street behind brick walls or iron fences. Stoiberhof, the Crawford Hill mansion, and the old Bonfils mansion formerly at the corner of 10th and Humbolt are examples of this new architecture for the rich. Complexity, vitality, exuberance, and wit had been replaced by an architecture reflecting fear, a desire for safety, and responsibility. Denver had in many ways retrenched for the battle against ruin and hysteria.[1]

PHOTO: EDWARDS AND BROWN

1070 Humbolt

The architecture of pre-crash Denver was in all probability the most significant architecture ever produced in this city, and it has been decimated by Denver's present building boom. Sherman Avenue and Grant Avenue, were deserted by the wealthy in the early twentieth century in favor of the newly developed Denver Country Club area and its neighboring regions in upper Capitol Hill. The old mansions near the Capitol signified the excesses and irresponsibility of the pre-crash ancestors, many of whom left after the crash and never returned. These old residences have been gradually torn down, giving way to apartment buildings, offices, and more recently parking lots or gas stations. Colfax Avenue, once among the most prestigious residential streets in Denver and the precursor of twentieth century streets like Sixth Avenue Parkway, has been altered beyond recognition. Almost all of Edbrooke's best and largest buildings are now gone, and the original Denver Club building has been replaced by a modern edifice with little real architectural character.

847 Pennsylvania

Sherman Avenue

The C. Haskell residence

Grant Avenue

A modest revival has, of course, begun, initiated by the private development of Larimer Square. Adventurous young Denverites have recently begun to follow suit in their attempts to revive lower downtown Denver, the heart of the original city and a section in which important buildings remain. The old National Block (First National Bank) still stands in very good condition at the corner of 15th and Blake Streets, and a remnant of the Brendlinger Building, the best commercial building built in Denver during the 1860's, remains intact under a sticky surface of pink stucco. The Oxford Hotel has been revived, and whole sections of what was the center of nineteenth century Denver are being bought and restored. Downtown Denver Incorporated, a group of merchants and professionals interested in the economic and historical future of that area, meets regularly, and the entire neighborhood is slowly beginning to nod after half a century of virtual sleep.

The Clayton Block

The Denver Cable Railway Co., 1889.

The old National Block

The Oxford Hotel

However, this attempt to restore or revive an entire area or neighborhood is not widespread. The neighborhoods around the Asbury Methodist Church, old Christ Methodist Church, Denver County Hospital, and Cheesman Park still maintain something of their nineteenth century character in spite of attempts to efface it. These areas should be zoned and revived as whole units before parking lots and high-rise apartment buildings intrude so far as to ruin them.

A citizenry of responsible and historically motivated individuals is beginning to emerge in Denver. Historic Denver Incorporated, an organization founded in 1970 and presently housed in an 1885 Second Empire house on 9th Street in Auraria, is one of the most active and effective private preservation groups in the country. Plans range in scope and character from the complete restoration of the Molly Brown House to the creation of a block park in what is left of Auraria, and are exciting and intelligent. The corporation's attempt to create a contingency fund designed to purchase endangered historic structures is not only commendable, but vital to the future of this city.

PHOTO: LULOW

The Moffat Mansion

The Molly Brown house

1015 9th Street

The Murat Cabin

Ninth Street

Tivoli Brewery buildings

The west has dissociated itself from its past for too many generations. Our fixation on the violent and the prurient aspects of nineteenth century western civilization is lamentable and has created a situation in which we feel moralistically superior to what are really mythical ancestors— our view of pre-crash Denver is confined too often to its madams, its saloons, its excesses, and its "Victorian" oddness.

It is time that we recognize the reality of nineteenth century Denver, a city of people who built homes, shopped in respectable stores, went to church, ran for the school board, and acted very much as we act today. Concededly less mobile and less attuned to the subtleties of international mass culture, they were nevertheless not intellectually isolated. Their architecture was not a sham; it was significant, varied, and exciting. Their affectations of "styles" from around the world must be seen in the light of our own fascination with styles— our apartment houses are built in affectations of "Florentine," Nordic, Mediterranean, French Provincial, and even Japanese. In many ways, we perceive less accurately than designers of the last century, and our persistent attempts to make styrofoam look like wood and plastic look like metal filigree are really no different from their attempts to mold metal into "stone" or coat plaster statues with bronze.

Our cultures are, in many ways, more similar than they are different. The vast expansion outward onto the great plains which has characterized the modern phenomenon of suburbia is in reality little different from the expansion which occurred in the nineteenth century. Isolated residential areas with curved streets were also built then, and the heavily roofed and very dark "rustic" houses now being built in southeast Denver have a strong resemblance to Denver developments of the late 1880's and early 1890's. Our interest in public transportation is not new but renewed, an interest which was pioneered by our ancestors who built a much better system of public transportation than we have today. The architecture of the so-called California

Union Depot

Denver

school which has begun to be evident in the 1970's is really not so different from the faceted masses of the architects' city built in Denver's greatest building boom. Even our interest in the townhouse, or condominium, is a revival of the terrace or walk-up which was a major form of domestic architecture around the turn of the century. The concept of downtown decentralization, a concept which in many ways has ruined present-day downtown Denver, was very alive in the nineteenth century; street-corner shopping centers with a market, a drug store, a penny candy shop, and, perhaps, a tavern or restaurant were built throughout the town and filled the immediate needs of Denverites. Downtown was special; it was bigger, better, more important, more modern, and more exciting than the neighborhood. Its dark theatres were filled with ornament from exotic cultures, and its restaurants had temptingly undomestic food.

Modern Denverites still have the opportunity to view the remnants of nineteenth century Denver with fresh eyes. Whole blocks and even neighborhoods could be revived and restored; new suburbs and buildings could

be built using the planning principles of the street and the viable neighborhood which underlie the nineteenth century city of Denver. The commuter train and the trolley are applicable to today's transportation problems. Awnings and street fixtures which enlivened the streets of downtown Denver in the nineteenth and early twentieth century Denver could re-appear or be redesigned, and the commitment to a beautiful city after dark which was so important to early Denverites could be made again. The possibilities are almost endless. All we need is a hefty dose of the civic pride and responsibility which characterized Denver in the last century, when buildings were widely publicized and citizens were more active in the future of their own city. Denver's city planners must be given the public and civic support necessary to save their work from condemnation as merely "visionary." Urban pride, America's growing commitment to the city, has a grand and important precedent in the nineteenth century city of Denver. The city of J.B. Dorman, the architects' city, should serve as a model to the new, excited Denverites.

17th Street at Union Depot

1439 Court Place

20th and Emerson Streets

Logan Avenue

16th Street

Cottrell Clothing Co.

The Denver Dry Goods Co.

Central Presbyterian Church

216

Ashland School

1642 Lawrence

The Majestic Building

The Albany Hotel

The Tabor Grand Opera House

The Broadway Theatre, Interior

Denver Tramway

Champa Street

Lakeside

Pennsylvania Avenue

Sherman Avenue

Washington Avenue

century and the advent of the inexpensive electric light were relatively unadorned. Signs were often carved into the face of the building or were placed in a position which was architecturally subordinate.

[7]The proper style name for these rather basic structures is an open question. Sandra Dallas, in her wonderfully racy history of Denver architecture, calls them "gothic." Though the houses do have what might be construed as a cathedral pitch to their eaves, this doesn't seem sufficient evidence for relating them to gothic. revival structures. The houses seem to be provincial versions of the cottages in the so-called bracketed style published in 1842 by Andrew Jackson Downing. They have almost no stylistic features which could be characterized as gothic and seem, in general, to be simply cottage types.

[8] Governor Gilpin's speech has a great deal of local notoriety and had been published in a number of nineteenth century histories of the region. Smiley is the only source which quotes the speech in full. (Smiley, pages 438 to 440.) Vickers also quotes it, though he omits the bulk of the speech and includes only the last paragraph. (Vickers, pages 184-185.)

The Founding of the City

The Railroad City

[1] Smiley, Jerome, *History of Denver*, Denver, 1901, p. 242.

[2] Most of the information about Denver's early cabins is derived from Smiley's 1901 *History of Denver*. His account is found principally in Chapter XXIII, pages 224-236. The information is often contradictory and the various claims of this or that cabin to have been the first cabin are treated in scrupulous detail. This problem is of little interest to the historian of architecture, and I have used Smiley's information only where it seems to apply to specific buildings and their mode of construction. Much of the factual information in this chapter is derived from Smiley, who remains the most detailed and valuable local historian available.

[3] Brick was probably the most important of local building materials throughout the nineteenth century. The *Western Architect and Building News* printed several articles on brick manufacturing, both locally and nationally, and Denver's own brick as well as the better known "golden brick" were favorite building materials of architects and contractors well into the twentieth century. Brick manufacture in the city and the local region needs a careful and comprehensive history. Its early use as a building material in Denver makes it one of the only quintessentially "Denver" features of local architecture, a feature which continues throughout all the styles and periods of the city's growth.

[4] The church gained some measure of national prominence at a much later date. It was published in the small but influential *Cyclopedia of Methodism* written by Matthew Simpson in 1881. Its rather blocky gothic solidity was thought worthy of a small church in the west, and it was used as an illustration of the fact that Methodism had conquered even the wild west.

[5] Some portion of the Brendlinger building still remains, though the corner portion has been torn down. Attempts should be made to save, restore, or even rebuild the structure which featured so prominently in nineteenth century views of the city. The Brendlinger building was probably the most beautiful and the most often photographed building constructed in Denver in the 1860's. It is presently covered with a relatively thick coat of pink stucco and its round-arched windows have been replaced with rectangular windows.

[6] Signs were not nearly as important to the nineteenth century Denverite as they are today. Buildings until the turn of the

[1] The most comprehensive account of Denver's first real estate boom is given in Smiley's *History of Denver* on pages 454 and 455. His details are sketchy, but fascinating, and his lack of precise documentation is countered by his extremely lively prose style.

[2] The *Denver Directory* of 1873 lists Charles F. Abony, Anthony Emmet, Lewis and Bancroft, J.L. Mitchell, John Moncrief, and W.H.J. Nichols as architects and superintendents. Of these initial architects, only Emmet and Nichols were to remain in the city for more than three years. The directories for 1873 and also for 1874 were unique in listing the total construction in the city as well as all the prominent buildings constructed in that year—1873, which was information from the previous year, saw the construction of $623,400.00 worth of brick buildings and $797,230.00 of frame buildings, and 1874 represented a jump with $967,100.00 of brick construction and $415,500.00 of frame construction. The tendency to build exclusively in brick or stone increased as the decade of the 1870's continued. By the later 1880's, virtually every building in the city was built of brick or stone, and brick replaced frame as the low cost building material.

[3] The whole question of the role of the architect in construction has very few clear answers for lack of any serious research in the field. In general, it seems that Denver architects of the 1870's were involved in ornamental design. They used either vernacular massings or pattern book massings onto which they applied mass produced details like wrought iron balconies, cornices, or metal columns. Their buildings were generally unique insofar as the combination of standardized details was unique. Architects were not involved either with intentional combinations of disparate styles or with massing until the latter 1870's and into the 1880's. Their role was almost exclusively the design of ornament.

[4] The only careful treatment of the Second Empire in print is in Henry Russell Hitchcock's invaluable *Architecture: Nineteenth and Twentieth Centuries* (Penguin, 1958). He confines his

discussion to the large civic, governmental, and institutional buildings constructed in that style and what he terms "Cognate Modes" throughout Europe. His discussion of the United States is limited, necessarily, to the most important and obvious Second Empire buildings. He omits a discussion of provincial variants of the style and its introduction as a major influence on ornamental design in the United States. Though there were few buildings constructed in the west which are purely Second Empire, the style seems to have given impetus to a more or less neo-Baroque sensibility which, when combined with the patterned detail of the Stick Style (Scully, 1955) or the so-called bracketed mode, gave new ornamental life to the cities of the American west. Denver's use of the Second Empire was decidedly less "gingerbready" than San Francisco's or Portland's, and the relative inaccessibility of wood for ornamental detail made Denver's reliance on the bracketed mode less intense than it was on the west coast. In general Denver architecture made a greater use of metal than wood for ornamental purposes. Denver's architecture was, therefore, more heavily reliant on the mass produced ornament from the east coast than it was on a tradition of local craftsmanship which was so evident in San Francisco.

[5] On provincial buildings of relatively small size, the mansard roof served not only to unify the building, but to miniaturize it. Prime examples are the group of Second Empire residences on 9th Street in Auraria now being restored by Historic Denver Incorporated. These houses which appear, both in photographs and in reality, to be small cottages are actually quite large, often consisting of over 2000 square feet. The mansard roof, which slants discreetly back from the street, and the cornice, which shrinks the apparent size of the second floor, serve to compact the house as an illusionistic object. The rooms under the eaves— often four bedrooms, an antechamber, a bathroom, and a staircase hall— are treated as secondary space, as space "under the eaves," and often don't enter into the viewer's comprehension of the house as a set of rooms.

[6] The required order and surface organization of the Second Empire facade saved many buildings of that style from diffuseness. The compositional rules were almost unbelievably simple and applicable to very primitive architecture. Architects of varying abilities and strengths as composers could and did design successful and well-composed Second Empire structures. The style was characterized by elements which served to unify or objectify buildings. It was a style which accented the center and which avoided diffuseness at all costs.

The Architects' City

chain of great civilizations which stretched imaginatively back to the Greeks. Pagan and Christian civilizations were included in the list, which seemingly had no ideological bias whatsoever. Historical thinking in the late nineteenth century and in the west was as eclectic as the architecture which we are about to discuss. Men of nineteenth century Denver had a global outlook, not a merely national outlook. Their minds stretched across the earth and back into time with equal abandon.

[2] It is possible to read some of the rocky buildings of downtown Denver as man-made mountains. The Granite Hotel, formerly the MacNamara Dry Goods Company, at the corner of 15th and Larimer Streets is an example of a building which was intended to evoke the mountains in all their mineral wealth. The exterior is covered with several different kinds of stone, all from the Colorado region, which are combined to form an image of almost unparalleled solidity and visual strength. The desire for compact forms, for forms which looked like rock crystals, rock cliffs, and boulders, animated a great deal of Denver architecture in the 1880's (the Granite Hotel was completed in 1882). Rusticated stone was intended to look natural rather than man-made, and it was to give the surface of a building a compacted and intensified rockiness. Even the stained glass windows on the interior of the Granite Hotel are designed to look like colored boulder fields. The imagery of nineteenth century Colorado architecture is often more complex than the modern viewer imagines. Buildings were intended to compete with the mountains; they were men's mountains, and their strong and severe shapes must be seen in this light. An analysis of this archeological or mineral interpretation of much Colorado architecture in the eighties would need a careful reading of the great mass of secondary literature on cities and on architecture which was produced in the state. This study could be very rewarding to the careful scholar and could be an exemplary study in the relationship between man and nature in one of the greatest periods of environmental encroachment in the history of civilization.

[3] It is interesting to speculate on the reasons for this omission of the architectural profession from biographical considerations. Nineteenth century Colorado was obsessed with biography. Hardly a local or state history exists without lengthy biographies of the area's most important and/or wealthy citizens. Architects were left out of these biographical essays with a singular persistence. The profession simply must not have been considered a profession in spite of the success and the quality of its productions. Denverites must have considered the architects of the late eighties to have been little different from their pattern-book predecessors.

[4] Jesse B. Dorman emerges as one of the most interesting men in the history of nineteenth century Denver. He came to Denver sometime in November of 1881 and remained there until 1902. In the intervening years, he worked for the *Denver Republican*, was editor of the Inter-Ocean, founded a publication called The Play, and founded and edited the *Western Architect and Building News*. He, like many of the architects whom he championed, seems to have avoided the biographical eye of nineteenth century historians. The listings of his name in the *Rocky Mountain News* are not at all significant. We learn that he suffered from timidity and stage-fright (*Rocky Mountain News,* April 24, 1883) and that he admired Eugene Field. But nothing more significant is recorded. He moved with an uncommon frequency, usually once a year, and must have been a bachelor. His life seems to have been sporadic and uneven. His listings in the *Denver Directory* display a man who either could not or would not keep a steady job or a steady place of residence. He is often listed with no occupation or simply as "editor" of no particular publication. His career needs to be looked into by some intrepid local historian. If he had done nothing but publish the *Western Architect and Building News,* he would have been among the most important nineteenth century Denverites.

[5] Western Architect and Building News, Volume 1, No. 1, p. 1.
[6] Ibid.
[7] Ibid.
[8] Ibid. No. 2, p. 15.
[9] A great deal of local architectural history remains to be done in this area. The precise role of draftsmen and assistants in the larger firms needs to be explored. Their training and their relationship to the city as well as to the office for which they worked needs examination.

[1] A study of the rhetoric of early Denver has yet to be done and would make an interesting small book. Many of the speeches, booklets, and newspaper articles are characterized by an almost appalling optimism and cultural excitement. The historical awareness of Denver's early citizens seems to have been simultaneously broad and superficial. The concept of the destiny of civilization in general, a concept which is almost never voiced in twentieth century society, was common in the later nineteenth century, especially in the west. Denver and the other western American cities were considered to be the latest great links in a

[10] Another vital and fruitful area for the historian or the artist interested in nineteenth century culture is the role of the photographer in the documentation of a place. Photographers' studios should be sorted out; volumes of their photographs should be re-published; and exhibitions of their work should be more frequent and better researched. These men are vital in establishing the image of the city. The character of their work, their precise sensibilities as artists and as citizens, and their motivations for doing the work they did could better aid the people of Denver in interpreting their productions. A photographer like McClure was a tireless recorder. He looked into homes, recorded the exteriors of all the important new structures, took genre scenes of Denverites about their daily life, flattered our incipient parks with well-chosen views, and photographed the panorama. W.H. Jackson was more of a regional rather than a metropolitan photographer. His *oeuvres* include thousands of photographs of the Rockies and the southwest and fewer photographs of the city of Denver. He was not really an "urban" photographer, a photographer who spent his life capturing a city. The work of these fine artists, and, in many ways, they were better than the painters of the region in those same years, has been unrecognized for too many years. Their careers should be resurrected so that Denverites can learn as much as possible about the nineteenth century city.

[11] *Symposium,* the journal of the Colorado chapter of the American Institute of Architects.

Frank E. Edbrooke

[1] Frank E. Edbrooke, *Frank E. Edbrooke,* privately printed, Denver 1918. All biographical information about Frank Edbrooke derives from his autobiography written in his later years and published privately in 1918. The single known copy of this little book is on deposit in the Colorado State Historical Society, Edbrooke's last building which was completed in 1915. The book is not notable for its literary achievement nor for its character insight. Edbrooke spent the greatest percentage of his literary energy on retelling his Civil War experiences and detailing his post-retirement trips to Panama and California. The section on his architecture contains a random list of his larger buildings and a vague approximation of the cost of all his structures. There are no details of his office, the nature of his partnership with Marean, or his role in the design process.

[2] Both the Tabor Buildings were designed in W.J. Edbrooke's office in Chicago. The elder Edbrooke remained in Chicago after the designs were completed and sent his younger brother Frank to over-see construction. W.J. Edbrooke did come to Denver in 1881, but left the city after an unsuccessful three years in 1884.

[3] Field's quip was printed in the *Denver Tribune.* A copy of the article appears in the H.A.W.–E.B. Tabor unpaginated Scrapbook II, Tabor Manuscripts, Colorado State Historical Society.

[4] Edbrooke did execute the murals for Tabor's personal suite. The murals, which must have horrified Oscar Wilde when he stayed there in 1882, were called simply "Allegory of the Arts" and have (perhaps fortunately) been destroyed.

[5] Though it may seem strange to the modern viewer to count window types in a building, the information is very useful. Commercial architects of the 1870's were concerned with individualizing every part of the buildings which they designed. They therefore used a variety of mail-order details which greatly increased the cost of the structure. Commercial design of the 1880's was more standardized in response to the much larger building programs. Architects like Edbrooke were somewhat in advance of their time in the simplification of detailing. In spite of its fabled opulence, the Tabor Grand Opera House was an extremely regularized structure for its date. The banding of the windows into groups and the use of a standardized window type were considerably in advance of the contemporary Windsor Hotel.

[6] After 1881, Edbrooke's partner in F.E. Edbrooke and Company was a man named Charles Marean, about whom nothing is recorded. Edbrooke's own writings as well as the literature about nineteenth century Denver architecture suggest that he himself was more than an architect solely interested in the problems of design. He was a businessman whose jovial presence was much sought after in Denver society. He was known as a big drinker, a seasoned party-goer, something of a gourmet, and a womanizer. There was also the predictable "other side" of his character: Mason, churchgoer, and faithful friend. All in all, Edbrooke's personality was ideal for an architect in a burgeoning, self-consciously important city. He was ambitious and hard-working, and even the parties and the drinking with cronies must be seen in terms of his career as a builder. He gave shape to people's dreams, and he taught Denver's wealthiest citizens to concretize their fortunes in prestigious "downtown."

[7] George B. Post's Mills Building in New York City built between 1881 and 1883 was the most notable example of an early use of the frontal light well.

[8] This conjoining of the arch and the gable was possibly derived from the well-known Bank of Commerce Building in Minneapolis designed by Harry W. Jones and completed in 1888.

[9] The problem of attributing a building from a fairly large office continues to plague architectural historians and critics. Edbrooke undoubtedly hired at least three draftsmen in addition to Marean, his partner. The activities of these men are not known. Edbrooke may or may not have been responsible for the final designs of his later buildings. It is probable that he designed the general massing and designated the materials for each new project and allowed his draftsmen to design the details and, perhaps, the entrance feature. Several talented architects worked in Edbrooke's office in their early years in Denver– Huddart, Hale, and Sterner, among them. These men probably carried a great deal of the design responsibility. Their precise role in the project cannot, however, be determined. The relative consistency of Edbrooke's architecture in both style and quality are probably sufficient evidence that Edbrooke himself maintained enough control over the design process to be credited with the bulk of his buildings. I shall avoid trying to attribute certain buildings or certain features of buildings to one or another of Edbrooke's known draftsmen.

[10] The influence of this small office building by Richardson on American commercial architecture of the early eighties is probably greater than has been supposed. It was a well-published structure and was very widely known in America. Its division of the main facade into an arcade with two flanking towers was simpler and grander than the normal Second Empire program with a central tower, and it had an undoubtable effect on the simpler commercial architecture of the west and mid-west.

[11] The exceptions to this rule– the Kittredge Block by Stuckert, the Baérresens' Mack Block, and the Pioneer Building — were among the most confusing and wobbly structures built in Denver's downtown. The very nervous character of the surface relief detracted from the clear structural imagery of these buildings and weakened them considerably. Of these three buildings, only the Kittredge Building stands today, and the remodeling of its first two floors has even further eroded its visual strength. The building should be restored to its former character. The only other notable building downtown which was finished with rusticated stone was the unattributed Ghost Building at the corner of 15th and Glenarm Streets. This building– which is

possibly by William Lang— is small and grandly designed, and its surface rhythm is held in check. Though in less than perfect condition, the Ghost Block is among the best nineteenth century commercial structures which remains in Denver's downtown.

[12] Another small change which markedly altered the building's appearance was the removal of the stone cornice between the third and fourth floors. This vital break between the base of the building and its arcade is missing, and the resulting merger of the sections is displeasing and seriously lessens the building's visual strength. The bases of the pilasters from the arcade level now float freely and greatly mar the apparent structure of the facade.

[13] Edbrooke's Richardsonian tendencies were probably strengthened and perhaps even spawned by his colleague Franklin Kidder. Kidder was trained in Boston and practiced architecture in that city between 1882 and 1888, when he came to Denver. His architecture was not consistently Richardsonian; however, there are several structures, notably the Asbury Methodist Church of 1890-91, which show a decisive Richardsonian influence. His knowledge of Richardson's architecture was undoubtedly first-hand, and he must have communicated a great deal of information and perhaps also photographs to other architects in Denver. The similarity between the Asbury Methodist Church and the Central Presbyterian Church is indicative of a connection between the two men. It is difficult, however, to explain Edbrooke's Richardsonianism in terms of Kidder. While Kidder's massing and plans are often derived from Richardson sources, his handling of details is more derivative of the Shingle Style and, on occasion, High Victorian Gothic than is Edbrooke's. A connection between the two men undoubtedly existed, but the exact nature of that connection cannot be detailed without more biographical information and more secure dating of the buildings involved.

[14] The Palladian-classical revial in American architecture of the 1880's is a complex subject which has not been systematically studied. The use of the tripartite "Palladian" window was common in domestic architecture of the east coast in the early eighties. This motif does not appear with any frequency in Denver architecture until much later in the decade and often not until the 1890's. The reason for this delay is obscure. Denver architects were "up-to-the-minute" designers in many ways by the 1880's and displayed in their designs a secure knowledge of the eastern and midwestern architecture which they chose to emulate. It seems unusual that they delayed in the use of neo-classical motifs. Perhaps the hints of sobriety and institutional order associated with Palladianism and Neo-Classicism in the 1880's were not admired in the self-made world of Denver.

two notable gothic churches of this period, Lang's St. Mark's and Kidder's Grace Methodist Church, are decidedly more eclectic and relate more clearly to provincial Victorian architecture than they do to the movement which began in the 1840's and 1850's in England. Only Harry Wendel's small chapel for the Fairmount Cemetary matches the Evan's Chapel in delicacy of detail. Its stylistic impetus is more decidedly French Gothic of the very late perpendicular variety and cannot be related to the Victorian Gothic of England in the nineteenth century.

[2] This comparison raises a problem in architectural connoiseurship. The Molly Brown house was built in 1890, the same year as the Everts house next door. The detailing of the wall and the staircase motif is almost identical in both houses. The materials and scale of the houses are also remarkably similar. Is it possible, therefore, that William Lang designed the hitherto unattributed Brown house? The answer is complex and the issue, for this critic, is unresolvable. In spite of the similarities mentioned above, the Molly Brown house shares none of the architectural complexity and the stylistic disjunctions which are so marked in the Everts house. It is a more characteristic Queen Anne street house with all the key features— paneled gable, pinwheel plan, and half-timbering. A secure attribution to William Lang would be very risky without further documentary evidence.

[3] There are at least four other rowhouses which can be tentatively ascribed to Lang. The pair at 1732 and 1734 Ogden Street relate very closely to the Washington Street group in their massing, detailing, and composition, and the tops of the rowhouses hidden behind 621 Colfax have a definitely Langian flavor. They are capricious, rusticated, active and, one might say, elfin.

[4] The text of this description was probably written by either William Lang or his partner, Marshall Pugh. Lang used these building lists published in every issue of the *Western Architect and Building News* as free advertisement. Instead of merely listing his buildings, their materials, and costs like other architects, he described his homes with enough detail to excite any reader to build a William Lang house.

[5] Nineteenth century Denver architects were often involved in speculative design— often under their own names and, at other times, as partners of reputable local construction firms. It was not uncommon in Denver during the building boom which we are discussing to build a group of two or three houses at the same time. Often the owners of a new house wanted to build a speculative group for their friends and prospective neighbors. This practice accounts for the "Lang groups" which are found throughout upper Capitol Hill, and, possibly, in other sections of Denver.

William Lang

Robert S. Roeschlaub

[1] The most notable and the earliest of the High Victorian churches in Denver is the Evans Chapel which has been moved to its present site on the Denver University campus. This small building is among the most elegant and attractive churches built in Colorado. It was completed in 1878, and is probably the best small building constructed in the city during that decade. Its delicacy of scale and the supreme competence and almost Puginian quality of its detail suggest that it was by an eastern or even an English architect. Its progeny in Denver are very few. The

[1] Mr. Kenneth Fuller of Fuller and Fuller, the successor firm of Roeschlaub and Fuller, has been of inestimable help in providing the author with biographical and architectural information about the architect. Most information in this chapter originated in his office and he generously allowed the author to read the manuscript of his article about the firm for *Symposia,* the publication of the western mountain region of the American Institute of Architects.

[2] Roeschlaub remains the only major architect of Colorado who

persistently avoided the predominant styles in American architecture during his career. His Richardsonian architecture is really Second Empire architecture with some Richardsonian details and features. His Second Empire architecture of the late 1870's and early 1880's shows a considerable variety. This does not mean, however, that his architecture was totally consistent and displayed no internal development. The difference between his schools of the early eighties and those of the later eighties is striking indeed. But this difference probably stemmed more from the lavishness of the commission than it did from any aesthetic change on the architect's part. In general, his architecture seems to have been concerned with complex movement, with halls, staircases, and towers. Though he used different means at different times, his planning principles were reasonably consistent in spite of the changes in his "style."

[3] The major source for lists of the architect's buildings is again Fuller and Fuller. These lists are based on several sources, the most important of which is the architectural drawings in the possession of the firm. Buildings from the 1870's are very rarely documented by architect, and Roeschlaub's career in that decade is as mysterious as any architect's in the city.

[4] This clarity of organization, which reaches its peak in University Hall and the Corona School, is not at all present in Denver University's Iliff School of Theology which I have attributed tentatively to Edbrooke. That building, like almost all of Edbrooke's other institutional buildings, was based on another building, often of a different functional type, somewhere else in the United States. The building has an imagery which relates to other architecture rather than to its immediate function, a remark which is not applicable to University Hall or Roeschlaub's schools of the later eighties or early nineties.

[5] Robert Roeschlaub's career seems to have been affected by the slump in construction and real estate speculation which characterized Denver of the mid-eighties. His commissions for the Denver Public Schools were grouped at the beginning and at the end of the decade, and he did no buildings for District Number 1 in either 1885 or 1886. His advertisements in the *Denver Directory* of 1888 and 1889 relied substantially on pictures of his work of the earlier part of the decade.

Denver did not develop an exciting and unique brand of local architecture in the middle eighties as did Minneapolis and Chicago. The two older cities did not have slumps in their building booms in that part of the decade and, as a result, eclipsed the smaller city of Denver in the quality and quantity of their architecture. Denver's architectural development was hurt to a great extent by this break in construction campaigns. Good architecture does not develop easily in a situation of quick booms and short depressions. Many architects who had offices for several years in Denver during the early eighties left the city in 1885, and the towering figures of Roeschlaub and Edbrooke were the only major continuities between Denver's architectural community of the early 1880's and that of the later 1880's.

sonian. One building ascribed to the firm which still stands in Manitou Springs, Briarhurst, is markedly less Richardsonian. It exhibits features derived from cottage architecture of the 1850's as well as the architecture of Norman Shaw. The handling of the stone and the treatment of the main facade is decidedly Richardsonian, and the house emerges as among the most eclectic buildings designed by a Denver architect in the nineteenth century. Briarhurst is dated 1888-89 and may have been the firm's last really eclectic building.

[2] Precise details about Huddart's early career are not available. His surviving daughter does not recall the name of her father's school, and his obituary in the *Denver Post* gives no specific mention of his training.

[3] J.J. Huddart's early eclecticism is understandable in view of his training and his career. His exposure to English architecture in one of its liveliest periods and his probable knowledge of the more abandoned colonial variants of European architecture in Brazil and Australia provided him with a decidedly unprincipled visual education. This "training," when combined with the almost extravagant eclecticism of Denver society in the 1880's, is ample justification for a stylistically inconsistent career. Huddart's knowledge of architecture was not traditional, based on a secure and detailed study of the thirty or forty greatest buildings of the western European world from the Greeks to the Renaissance. Rather, his knowledge was based on training as an engineer and his exposure to a wide variety of unofficial architecture. The colonial architecture of Brazil and Australia is, like almost all colonial architecture, an architecture of imagery, an architecture which attempts to connect itself with the motherland or, at best, improve on the architecture of the motherland. J.J. Huddart's knowledge of this colonial architecture and his subsequent move to Denver, a colony with no clearly defined motherland, created a situation in which a steady and principled career would have been almost totally impossible.

[4] *Architecture,* J.J. Huddart, printed privately, Denver, 1907, no pagination.

[5] The parsonage for the Central Presbyterian Church was published in the November 1, 1890 issue of the nation's most important architectural journal, the *American Architect and Building News.* The fact that Kidder's building was published over the work of better local architects probably related to his eastern training and his circle of friends in Boston.

[6] Franklin Kidder, *Churches and Chapels,* New York, 1895, p. 6.

[7] Ibid.

[8] The best source for biographical information about the Baerresen brothers is V.E. Baerresen's son, H.H. Baerresen, who currently resides in Denver. Mr. H.H. Baerresen has been an exemplary recorder of his father's as well as his uncle's career together. He has saved newspaper articles, photographs of their buildings, letters, plans, and office records. He was very kind in allowing me to peruse this information on several occasions.

Eclecticism

Richardsonianism

[1] This remark is applicable probably only because the careers of these two excellent architects are so little known. All the surviving buildings by Varian and Sterner are notably Richard-

[1] *American Architect and Building News,* Feb. 17, 1877, p. 50.

[2] Though the terminology of this chapter is irritatingly unclear, some attempt has been made to use the words "Richardson" and

"Richardsonian" accurately. A building which is *derived* from a building by H.H. Richardson is called Richardsonian. This is clear enough, but the problem comes when a Richardsonian building which is *not* derived from a building in the master's career presents itself. Although Richardsonianism was *generally* a style which was counter to eclecticism, even it was eclectic. Because architects in the nineteenth century used so many models for their buildings, they often copied copies of copies. This tendency, which is basic to eclectic architecture, was also very active in Richardsonian architecture. This chapter will attempt to sort out some of the strands and varieties of the movement which has been called "Richardsonianism." This movement was by far the dominant stylistic movement in the western United States throughout the 1880's. An analysis of the variety in "Richardsonian" buildings will aid in our understanding of the provincial architecture of this great western city. Scholarly work on the movement has been almost non-existent in recent years. Buildings which derive from a model in Richardson's career have often been condemned as "derivative" when, in fact, all nineteenth century architecture, all architecture, is derivative. A more serious catalogue of Richardsonian buildings needs to be made before the definitive study of the style can be written.

[3] Another important aspect of Richardsonian influences in Denver was the city's competition with the larger and older twin cities, Minneapolis and St. Paul. Thanks to the firms of Leroy Buffington and Long and Kees, Minneapolis had been a predominantly Richardsonian city since 1885. Its houses and office structures, many of which have been savagely destroyed in recent years, bore a remarkable similarity to the architecture of Denver built between 1888 and 1892. The massive wall and the same rusticated stone obsessed the architects of both cities, and Denver architects acknowledged the superiority of Minneapolis architecture as late as 1889 in the *Western Architect and Building News.* Indeed, Denver's connection with Minneapolis seems to have been fruitful and important, perhaps even more important than Denver's aesthetic dependence on Chicago. Lack of any major scholarly work on either city has made a study of provincial Richardsonian architecture in America very difficult. Scholars have concentrated on the weaker Richardsonianism of the east and, curiously, of Europe before tackling the thornier but more interesting issue of Richardsonianism and provincial architecture in the western United States. The major work done on Richardsonian architecture in the west remains a two-part article by Montgomery Schuyler already referred to: "Glimpses of Western Architecture." These two articles— on Chicago and Minneapolis-St. Paul— are the most valuable contribution to the study of Richardsonianism in the west, but they are little more than lists with provocative critical comments. Schuyler, like any tough critic, states which buildings are good and which buildings are bad without really analyzing their sources in Richardson's and Richardsonian work.

[4] Fred J. Sterner came to Denver in 1882 and worked for one year as a draftsman for F.E. Edbrooke and Company. In 1883, he was listed as an independent architect with offices at 293 16th Street. E.P. Varian also came to Denver in 1882, but he was not listed in connection with any particular firm and seems to have been a "free-lance" draftsman. He, like Sterner became an independent architect in 1883 with a large-letter listing in the *Denver Directory:* "E.P. Varian and Co., 34 Tabor Block." The office at 34 Tabor Block was immediately down the hall from the prominent offices of F.E. Edbrooke and Company, and the two architects undoubtedly knew each other. Sterner probably came to work for Varian in 1884 and joined the partnership in 1885, Varian and Sterner, 34 Tabor Block. The listing for that year was in small letters and indicates that the new partnership was not prospering in the construction slump. Varian and Sterner perservered, however, and by 1889, they had the commission for the Denver Club, the city's first Richardsonian building to be featured in the *Western Architect and Building News.*

Epilogue

[1] Denver architecture did not really recover its vigor and strength until after the First World War, when a new breed of architects trained in Europe and well versed in the various architectural "styles" began to redesign Denver. Most of their memorable creations were extravagant houses for post-crash Denverites, houses which cluster around the Denver Country Club and dot the corners of lower Capitol Hill. These dwellings, designed by Arthur K. Fisher, J.J. Benedict, Lester Varian, and many others, still dominate Denver's real estate market and have continued to maintain their status as the city's most prestigious homes. These buildings need study and documentation before they too become the remnants of an almost unknown local past.

Bibliography

Bibliography

The source material immediately relevant to Denver's architecture of the nineteenth century is somewhat meager. The best sources are the photograph collections of the Western History Department at the Denver Public Library as well as the Colorado State Historical Society. Those vast collections are uncatalogued and difficult for the amateur to use.

This bibliography does not include material which is not relevant to Denver, as good bibliographies of nineteenth century American architecture are available in published sources. The reader is directed to Henry Russell Hitchcock's monumental *Architecture: Nineteenth and Twentieth Centuries* (Penquin, 1958, 3rd edition) for the most complete general bibliography. Carl Condit's *The Chicago School of Architecture* (University of Chicago Press, 1964) includes a bibliography which stresses the west and the middle west.

Perhaps the most valuable collection of American architectural writings of the nineteenth century is *The Literature of Architecture: The Evolution of Architectural Theory and Practice in Nineteenth Century America* (E.P. Dutton and Company, 1966) edited by Don Gifford. These three sources will immerse the reader in all aspects of nineteenth century architectural studies.

This bibliography also omits the vast scholarly and popular studies done on so-called "frontier" or "pioneer" history. The culture of the early American west has produced a considerable body of this literature, a great deal of which is exaggerated and unscholarly. The view of the pioneer which was propagated so widely in the last century is being revised in light of recent studies, and this author has not maintained an up-to-the-minute knowledge of that bibliography.

American Architect and Building News. This national architectural magazine contained sporadic mentions of Denver and her architecture. They are as follows: 1880 (Jan.-June), pages 49 and 133, competition for courthouse; 1880 (July-Dec.), page 129, courthouse competition; 1881 (Jan.-June), pages 145, 154, and 169, report of the fall of a building (court case in which Eberley is cleared); 1881 (July-Dec.), pages 165 and 184, fall of the Strauss Building; page 307, glass making in Morrison; 1883 (July-Dec.), pages 2 and 37, Denver Capitol competition; 1884 (July-Dec.), page 70, Denver Chamber of Commerce competition; 1885 (Jan.-June), page 213, Denver Capitol competition; 1885 (July-Dec.), pages 49 and 103, Denver Capitol competiton; 1891 (Jan.-June), page 195, fireproof arches for the Equitable Building.

Architectural Bibliography, lists of books on architecture in the Denver Public Library, 1924.

Architects,' Contractors,' and Material Dealers' Directory for the State of Colorado, 1892. This valuable catalogue contains mostly advertisements, but is an enormous help in understanding the relative sophistication of the building trade in the state during the building boom. It can be found in the Western History Department of the Denver Public Library.

Arps, Louisa Ward, *Denver in Slices,* Sage Books, Denver, 1959. A good, clear, entertaining, and well-illustrated set of mini-histories of Denver— Elitches, Tabors, Baron Richthofen, the Windsor Hotel, etc.

Baerresen, H.W. and V.E., *Architectural Views,* privately printed, Denver, 1916. The best guide to the work of this firm. The booklet is in the possession of the Western History Department in the Denver Public Library.

Barber, John W., *The Loyal West,* E.A. Howe, publisher, Cincinatti, 1865. This large volume on the frontier west has a small section on Denver and an illustration of the town on page 739.

Barbot's Illustrated Guide to Denver, privately printed, Denver, 1891. One of the numerous guidebooks to the city published in the early nineties, in the Western History Department of the Denver Public Library.

Blackmore, William, *Colorado: Its Resources, Parks, and Prospects,* London, 1869. Several editions of this volume exist. It is illustrated with real photographs.

Brenneman, Bill, *Miracle on Cherry Creek,* World Press, Denver, 1973. This small book is the best history of a neighborhood or area of Denver yet written. It could serve as a model for the study of the city by areas, a scholarly task which should begin immediately.

City Club of Denver, *Art in Denver,* privately printed, 1928. This very slim volume describes the survival of the art and sketching clubs begun in Denver of the nineteenth century into the twentieth century.

The Coloradoan, an illustrated semi-monthly journal, Vol. I, No. 1, June 1, 1892. This short-lived periodical contained discussion of the new buildings, especially schools, built in the city in that year. It is indicative of the civic pride and the spirit of healthy criticism which animated the city in the early nineties.

Dallas, Sandra, *Cherry Creek Gothic,* University of Oklahoma Press, Norman, 1971. This essential source views the history of Denver architecture through the lens of Denver society, particularly its more exciting side. It is racy, interesting, and very well-illustrated.

Dallas, Sandra, *Gaslights and Gingerbread,* Sage Books, Denver, 1965.

Dallas, Sandra, *Gold and Gothic,* Lick Skillet Press, Denver, 1967. The definitive history of Larimer Square.

Davis, Sally and Baldwin, Betty, *Denver Dwellings and Descendants,* Sage Books, Denver, 1963. A geneological study of Denver with some architectural photographs.

Day, James Ingersoll, *Our Architecture and Scenes of Denver,* F.E. Edbrooke, architect, Denver, 1906. The most inclusive photographic survey of the works of Denver's greatest architect. The book's only annoying feature is that no dates are provided.

Debo, Angie, *Prairie City,* Knopff, New York, 1944.

Denver and its Outings, privately printed, Denver, 1890. A very small photographic guide to the city and its surrounding beauties. It indicates the connection between Denverites of the later nineteenth century and their mountainous environment.

Denver Picturesque and Descriptive, Art Publishing Company, Wisconsin, 1889. This is one of the three or four most important sources for architectural information about Denver in the later eighties. It is profusely illustrated and has an informative and well-printed text.

The Denver Republican, New Year Issue, January 1, 1873. This single issue of *The Denver Republican* is probably as valuable as any book ever written about Denver architecture. It was published several months before the crash and provides illustrations, attributions, descriptions, and discussions of the buildings recently completed or under construction in the city. It is the document for the end of the boom.

Duhem Brothers, photographers, *Picturesque Colorado,* Denver 1875. This small book is a collection of original photographs by the best Denver photographers of the 1870's. It is typical of the "city books" which were produced by nineteenth century photographers and sold to prominent citizens of the city. The most famous of these books were produced by W.H. Jackson, Denver's greatest photographer of the 1880's.

Edbrooke, Frank E., *Frank E. Edbrooke,* privately printed, Denver, 1918. The uninspired, but informative autobiography of Denver's most important architect. The single copy of this book survives in the library of the Colorado State Historical Society.

Etter, Don, *Auraria,* Colorado Associated University Press, 1972. This small picture book is the most sympathetic and moving book ever written on Denver architecture. The pictures are excellent, but there is little text. Mr. Etter writes clearly, intelligently, and compassionately.

Fosset, Frank, *Colorado Tourists' Guide,* C.G. Crawford, New York, 1880. Some good engravings of buildings in the city are included in this early guidebook. There are also a great many costs and dates for buildings constructed in the latter seventies. This book would be indispensible to any historian working on Denver in that decade.

Frank Leslie's Illustrated Newspaper, August 20, 1859, pages 183-186. Three views of early Denver are published in this issue.

Griswold, Don and Jean, *Colorado's Century of Cities,* Smith Brooks, printer, 1958. A relevant early history of the Colorado "cities" and the wild speculative activities of the later nineteenth century. Manifest destiny runs wild in this excellent book.

Harper's Weekly, October 13, 1866, page 644. A small article called "Life on the Plains" with sketches of Denver by James Gookins is one of the best indications that the plains west in the 1860's was respectable, unwild, and rather dull.

Huddart, John J., *Architecture,* privately printed, Denver, 1907. This small book, now in the possession of the architect's daughter, Mrs. Viola Westbrook, has photograhs of many Huddart buildings and remains the single means of attributing buildings to this excellent architect. A short prose passage by the architect himself at the end of the volume gives an outline of his life.

Jackson, Olga, *Mountains, Mines, and Mansions: An Architectural Guide to Colorado,* published for the American Institute of Architects, Denver, 1966. A short photographic guide to all Colorado architecture with brief and generally accurate attributions of nineteenth century buildings.

Jackson, W.H., *Denver Views,* photographs by Jackson, no text, Denver, circa 1890. This volume of photographs is Jackson's

view of the city comparable to that of the Duhem brothers in 1875. It is unique and remains in the Beinecke Rare Book and Manuscript Library at Yale University.

Kennedy, Roger G., *Men on the Moving Frontier,* American West Publishing, 1969.

Kohl, Edith Eudora, *Denver's Historic Mansions: Citadels to the Empire Builders,* Sage Books, Denver, 1957. A house by house description of some of Denver's major mansions. The photographs are good, but the text is more description than history.

Letham, J., *Historical and Descriptive Review of Denver, Her Leading Business Houses and Enterprising Men,* Denver, 1893 (?).

Mathews, A.E., *Pencil Sketches of Colorado,* 1866. The most famous illustrations of Colorado in the 1860's, Mathews' sketches were copies, replicated and pirated by hundreds of early illustrators of Colorado. Smiley in his definitive history of Denver disputes the accuracy of the sketches.

New York Illustrated News, October 4, 1862. View of Auraria in connection with an Indian massacre (as they were called). The text considers Auraria to be on the Minnesota plains.

Parsons, Eugene, *A Guidebook to Colorado,* Little Brown, Boston, 1914. A county by county guide to the state of Colorado, Parsons' book includes a lot of architectural information but few photographs.

Rister, Carl Coke, "The Settler's Home," *Southern Plainsman,* 1938, pages 58-69. A descriptive essay which is a good evocation of housing on the great plains throughout the nineteenth century and housing in Denver during the 1860's and early 70's.

Sandborn Map and Publishing Company, *Map of Denver, Colorado,* published for the Denver Board of Underwriters, New York, 1887. The most complete maps of Denver in 1887, the Sandborn maps show completed buildings on their lots and separate them into frame, brick, and stone.

Sanborn-Perris Map Company, *Insurance Maps,* Denver, Colorado, 1890-93, New York. The most complete nineteenth century maps of Denver.

Smiley, Jerome C., *History of Denver,* The Times-Sun Publishing Company, Denver, 1901. Smiley's history is the definitive history of Denver in the nineteenth century and is one of the great local histories published in the United States in the nineteenth century.

Smith, Thomas, L., *Denver Illustrated,* Denver Real Estate and Stock Exchange, Denver, 1893. Smith produced one of the best nineteenth century photo books with a great deal of real estate information.

Tonge, Thomas, *Denver by Pen and Pencil,* Thayer Publishing, Denver, 1898. The guidebook by the dean of Denver promoters in the nineteenth century. Tonge wrote about everything— buildings, social life, bricks, restaurants, etc.

Vickers, W.B., *History of the City of Denver, Arapahoe County, and Colorado,* O.L. Baskin and Company, Chicago, 1880. Vickers wrote a long and chatty history of the state, its resources and its principal citizens. The engravings are helpful and numerous.

The Western Architect and Building News, edited by J.B. Dorman, published in Denver between 1889 and 1892. The best source for architectural information ever produced.

The Western Magazine, published in Denver between 1877 and 1888.

Workers of the Writers Program (WPA), *Colorado, A Guide to the Highest State,* Hastings House, New York, 1941. This is an excellent guidebook with a concise and factual presentation, selected bibliography, and a chronology.

A Western Town Called Denver, privately printed, Denver, 1897. Another excellent local guidebook.

This bibliography is certainly not complete. It includes what this writer has found to be the most helpful sources in his study of nineteenth century architecture of the city. More general listings will be found in Sandra Dallas' *Cherry Creek Gothic* and Bill Brenneman's *Miracle on Cherry Creek.*

Index

Index

A

B

C

Q

Quayle, William, 123
Queen Anne style, features, 58; defined, 129; use by Lang in rowhouses, 80-85
Quincy Building (Edbrooke), 128

R

Race Street, 1457 (Lang), 89, 91; 1544 (Lang), *90*
Railroad, 8-19; competition for, 7; arrival of first locomotive in Denver, 8; effects on Denver, 8, 11, 19; as symbol of modernity, 11
Rainbow, J.R., competition drawing of country schoolhouse, *31*
Randall, G.E., Arapahoe School, 11-12, *12*
Raymond house (Lang), 64, *65-68,* 88
Rice, E.R., 30
Richardson, H.H., 21, 39, 40, 46, 150; index of illustrations: Allegheny County buildings, *163, 190;* Albany City Hall, *164;* Ames Building, *176;* Ames Gate Lodge, *155, 157;* Billings Library, *159;* Chamber of Commerce Building (Cincinnati), *162;* Crane Memorial Library, *157;* Glessner residence, *185;* Gratwick house, *193;* Marshall Field Warehouse, *151;* McVeagh house, *185;* Sever Hall, *160;* Sherman residence, *183;* Trinity Church, *166; see also* Richardsonianism
Richardsonianism, 64, 150-195; decorative motifs, 171, 180; definition, 54; as distinguished from Richardson's sources, 156; domestic, 182; *see also* Richardson, index of illustrations.
Richthofen Castle, 182, *182*
Rhodes residence (Edbrooke), *60,* 61
Rocky Mountain News, 2
Roeschlaub, Robert, 20, 27, 30, 31, 64, 94-121; arrival in Denver, 94; Ashland School, 94, 98, *217;* Central City

Opera House, 94, 96, *97,* 98, 100, 116; Central Presbyterian Church, 94, *96,* 115, 116; Chamberlin Observatory, *95,* 174, *174-175;* commercial architecture, 114-115 (*see also* building names); Corona School (Dora Moore School) 102, 106, 109, *106-109,* 110; Denver City High School, 27, 99, *99;* Ebert School, 30, 98, *98,* 109, *109,* 114; Emerson School, 100-101, *100-101;* Gilpin School, 98; Gottesleben residence, 94, *95;* Hyde Park School (Wyatt School), 102, *102;* King Block, 114; Longfellow School, 98; schools, 98-113; Times Building, 114-115; Trinity Methodist Episcopal Church, 96, 115-120, *115-121;* Union Block, 114-115, *114;* University Hall, 96, 109-110, *110-113,* 153, 174; Whittier School, 98; Wyman School, *103-105*
Ryerson Building, 39

S

St. Anthony's Hospital, 30
St. Charles, 1
St. James Methodist-Episcopal Church (Kidder), 140
St. Joseph's Hospital (Baerresen brothers), 30, 128
St. Luke's Hospital, 30
St. Mark's Church (Lang), 30, 64, 68-69, *68-69,* 70, 145
St. Mary's Academy, 16, *31*
Salt Lake City, Gus Holmes Building (Huddart), 135
Schleier residence (Edbrooke), 57, 58, *58,* 71
Second Empire, description of style, 13, *19*
Seventeenth Street, *214*
Sheridan Building (Baerresen brothers), 143, *144*
Sherman School, 180

Sherman Avenue, *202, 220*
Shingle Style, influence on domestic architecture, 21
Signs, placement on buildings, 5
Sixteenth Street, *216*
Skinner residence (Edbrooke), 57, 58, *58*
South Broadway Christian Church (Miller and Janisch), 152, 171, 177, *177-179,* 180
Spencer, John, drawing, *24*
Sterner and Varian, *see* Varian and Sterner
Stephens residence (Huddart), 132, *134*
Stoiberhof, 201
Stone, as replacement for brick in construction, 23, 31; use during 1880's, 46
Stout cabin, *2*
Stout, E.P., 1, 2
Stout Street School, 11, *12*
Street car system, failure, 31
Stuckert, Morris, 123, Beaumont residence, *27;* Kittredge Building, 26-27, 30
Sullivan, Louis, 39, 40; Chicago Auditorium, 30, 39, 42, 49, 48-49
Swedish Lutheran Church (Baerresen brothers), 144-145, *145*
Swift Building (Pueblo) (Huddart), 135, *135*

T

Tabor Block (Edbrooke), 19, 20, 33-35, *34*
Tabor Grand Opera House (Edbrooke), 19, 20, 33, 35-36, *36,* 37, 39, 42, 45, 61, 63, *218*
Tabor, H.A.W., influence on construction in Denver, 20, 33
Tappan Building, 9
Tedford residence (1415 Vine) (Lang), 80, *81-82*
Tenth Street, *235;* 1145
Third Congregational Church (Kidder), *141*